The Art and Craft of Comparison

Is it possible to compare French presidential politics with village leadership in rural India? Most social scientists are united in thinking such unlikely juxtapositions are not feasible. Boswell, Corbett and Rhodes argue that they are possible. This book explains why and how. It is a call to arms for interpretivists to embrace creatively comparative work. As well as explaining, defending and illustrating the comparative interpretive approach, this book is also an engaging, hands-on guide to doing comparative interpretive research, with chapters covering design, fieldwork, analysis and writing. The advice in each revolves around 'rules of thumb', grounded in experience, and illustrated through stories and examples from the authors' research in different contexts around the world. Naturalist and humanist traditions have thus far dominated the field but this book presents a real alternative to these two orthodoxies which expands the horizons of comparative analysis in social science research.

John Boswell is Associate Professor in Politics at the University of Southampton, UK. He is the author of *The Real War on Obesity* (2016).

Jack Corbett is Professor of Politics at the University of Southampton, UK. He is the author or editor of five books and more than sixty articles and book chapters. He holds honorary appointments at the Coral Bell School of Asia Pacific Affairs, the Australian National University, and the Centre for Governance and Public Policy, Griffith University, Australia.

R. A. W. Rhodes is Professor of Government (Research) at the University of Southampton, UK. He is the author or editor of 40 books and 200 articles and book chapters, most recently, *Network Governance and the Differentiated Polity. Selected Essays. Volume I*; and *Interpretive Political Science. Selected Essays. Volume II* (2017). He is a fellow of the Academy of the Social Sciences in Australia and the United Kingdom. In 2014, the Political Studies Association (PSA) awarded him its Special Recognition Award. In 2015, the European Consortium for Political Research (ECPR) awarded him their biennial Lifetime Achievement Award.

Strategies for Social Inquiry

This new book series presents texts on a wide range of issues bearing upon the
practice of social inquiry. Strategies are construed broadly to embrace the full
spectrum of approaches to analysis, as well as relevant issues in philosophy of social
science.

Published Titles

John Gerring, *Social Science Methodology: A Unified Framework*, 2nd edition
Michael Coppedge, *Democratization and Research Methods*
Thad Dunning, *Natural Experiments in the Social Sciences: A Design-Based Approach*
Carsten Q. Schneider & Claudius Wagemann, *Set-Theoretic Methods for the Social
    Sciences: A Guide to Qualitative Comparative Analysis*
Nicholas Weller & Jeb Barnes, *Finding Pathways: Mixed-Method Research for
    Studying Causal Mechanisms*
Andrew Bennett and Jeffrey T. Checkel, *Process Tracing: From Metaphor to Analytic
    Tool*
Diana Kapiszewski, Lauren M. MacLean and Benjamin L. Read, *Field Research in
    Political Science: Practices and Principles*
Peter Spiegler, *Behind the Model: A Constructive Critique of Economic Modeling*
James Mahoney and Kathleen Thelen, *Advances in Comparative-Historical Analysis*
Jason Seawright, *Multi-Method Social Science: Combining Qualitative and
    Quantitative Tools*
John Gerring, *Case Study Research: Principles and Practices*, 2nd edition

The Art and Craft of Comparison

John Boswell
University of Southampton

Jack Corbett
University of Southampton

R. A. W. Rhodes
University of Southampton

CAMBRIDGE
UNIVERSITY PRESS

CAMBRIDGE
UNIVERSITY PRESS

University Printing House, Cambridge CB2 8BS, United Kingdom

One Liberty Plaza, 20th Floor, New York, NY 10006, USA

477 Williamstown Road, Port Melbourne, VIC 3207, Australia

314–321, 3rd Floor, Plot 3, Splendor Forum, Jasola District Centre, New Delhi – 110025, India

79 Anson Road, #06–04/06, Singapore 079906

Cambridge University Press is part of the University of Cambridge.

It furthers the University's mission by disseminating knowledge in the pursuit of
education, learning, and research at the highest international levels of excellence.

www.cambridge.org
Information on this title: www.cambridge.org/9781108472852
DOI: 10.1017/9781108561563

© John Boswell, Jack Corbett and R. A. W. Rhodes 2019

First published 2019

Printed in the United Kingdom by TJ International Ltd, Padstow Cornwall

A catalogue record for this publication is available from the British Library.

Library of Congress Cataloging-in-Publication Data
Names: Boswell, John, 1983– author. | Corbett, Jack, 1985– author. | Rhodes, R. A. W., author.
Title: The art and craft of comparison / John Boswell, University of Southampton; Jack Corbett, University
    of Southampton; R.A.W. Rhodes, University of Southampton.
Description: Cambridge, UK; New York, NY: Cambridge University Press 2019. | Series: Strategies in
    social inquiry | Includes bibliographical references and index.
Identifiers: LCCN 2019013155 | ISBN 9781108472852 (hardback) | ISBN 9781108460668 (paperback)
Subjects: LCSH: Social sciences–Comparative method. | Social sciences–Research–Methodology.
Classification: LCC H61 .R4854 2019 | DDC 330.72/1–dc23
LC record available at https://lccn.loc.gov/2019013155

ISBN 978-1-108-47285-2 Hardback
ISBN 978-1-108-46066-8 Paperback

Contents

Tables

Acknowledgements

We wrote this book under the auspices of the Centre for Political Ethnography at the University of Southampton. We would like to thank Lorraine De Velo, Wouter Veenendaal, Matt Ryan and Reem Abou-El-Fadl for thoughtful comments on our initial proposal. The people who came to our paper at APSA 2017, especially discussants Fred Schaffer and Robin Turner, provided detailed feedback. We thank, Matt Wood, Paul 'tHart and Mark Bevir for reading and commenting on the final manuscript, and a special thank you to Paul for allowing us to quote him in the final text. Two anonymous reviewers also made helpful suggestions on the proposal and early draft chapters. For helpful discussions, we would like to thank Chris Chevalier John Cox, Ian Hall and Niheer Dasandi. As ever, John Boswell, Jack Corbett and Rod Rhodes thank Seahee Cho, Vanessa Corbett and Jenny Fleming for their love and support.

We are grateful to the following publishers for their permission to reprint extracts from: Taylor & Francis for Boswell, J. and Corbett, J. (2015) 'Embracing Impressionism: Revealing the Brush Strokes of Interpretive Research', Critical Policy Studies (9): 216-25; and Oxford University Press for Rhodes, R. A. W. (2011) *Everyday Life in British Government* Oxford: Oxford University Press.

1 Comparative Intuition

Is it possible to compare French presidential politics with, say, village level politics in rural India? The conventional wisdom in both naturalist comparative social science and humanist area studies is a resounding 'no'. Even if this comparison could reveal interesting insights, it would be impossible to design a study that would make methodological sense.

For naturalist social scientists, the main objection would be that the contexts are too different, irrespective of the variables we might choose to investigate (that is, institutions, economic development, political culture or religion). We might compare (say) Indian and French political systems at the national level, or small-town politics in France with village politics in rural India. But the scales of presidential politics and village politics are just too different. In fact, they are so different that they do not even conform to a 'most different' design (Lijphart 1971) because there is not even *one* variable that might link them. In other words, it is not like comparing apples with oranges; it is like comparing an elephant with an ant. Rather than varieties of fruit, they are different species.

Humanist area studies scholars would reach the same negative conclusion though using a different logic. Comparison, from this perspective, runs the risk of sacrificing rich, nuanced and context-bound insights on the altar of parsimony, generalisability and theoretical elegance. In this tradition, the concern is that these types of studies often contain inaccuracies and misunderstandings due to insufficient knowledge of the place under study. The point here is not that we cannot make this trade-off, but rather such an exercise would not produce meaningful insights.

The aim of this book is to present an alternative to these two common ways of seeing and studying the social world. French presidential politics and village politics in rural India may seem beyond meaningful comparison. But if we probe deeper, we begin to see that presidents and village leaders share common dilemmas – how to mobilise supporters, how to ensure the loyalty of allies, whether to weaken or placate rivals, how to manipulate crisis and survive scandal, whether to implement change or preserve the status quo. Indeed, when we think about politics in this actor-centred way, we start to realise that the comparison we propose is not as incongruous as first appeared. We might even begin to imagine a president and a village leader sitting down together and discussing political tactics and manoeuvres, sharing what works and what does not. Rather than having nothing to offer, the findings of such a study might turn out to be interesting, even illuminating. Indeed, such research might find that some presidents have more in common with counterpart village leaders than they do with other presidents.

This example is not a thought experiment. It echoes the logic of F. G. Bailey's (1969) classic *Stratagems and Spoils*. Context, for Bailey, was not a constraint, either methodologically or philosophically. Unlikely juxtaposition allowed him to render both the exotic familiar and the familiar exotic, opening space for thinking about politics as an essentially human activity in which we all take part. In doing so, he revealed *both* the universal and the particular; the dilemmas are similar but the strategies actors pursue and the consequences of their choices can be different (cf. Adcock 2006: 62).

The implications of this approach for how we undertake comparative research across the social sciences is potentially profound. As our brief illustration highlights, conventional wisdom about when, how and why to compare severely limits how we study and understand the social world. As a result, we are missing potentially rich and illuminating insights because our analysis is either too rigid, structured and systematic or too bespoke, detailed and idiographic. We seek to address these limitations – and expand the horizons of comparison – by outlining a novel, clear and sound approach to comparative interpretive analysis.

We are indebted in this pursuit not just to a long line of innovators like Bailey, but also to a recent eruption of interest in the means and ends of comparison in social science. For example, the late Benedict Anderson's (2016) memoir *A Life beyond Boundaries* challenges old presumptions about the practice and utility of small-n and medium-n research. Reflecting on his own career, and in particular on the slow-burning but spectacular success of *Imagined Communities* (1983), Anderson revels in the creative spark that enabled him to make 'surprising' but revealing comparisons across apparently disparate contexts. His approach bemused his naturalist colleagues in comparative politics, while his contemporaries in humanist area studies regarded it with caution.

While Anderson's reflections open new possibilities for comparative research, they are limited because he treats the work of making comparisons as a mysterious and indescribable form of alchemy. He provides no basis for different comparative strategies, and no guidance on how to conduct such research. This book seeks to demystify the process. Its chief contribution is to provide a philosophically sound and practically useful guide to a distinctively interpretive form of comparison.

In doing so, we contribute to fast-moving debates about the universal–particular divide. In recent times, these discussions have been dominated by naturalist social scientists seeking to defend the value of qualitative research (for example: Bennett and Checkel 2015; Blatter and Haverland 2012; Coppedge 2012; George and Bennett 2005; Gerring 2012a, 2017; Goertz 2006; Goertz and Mahoney 2012). But while we are sympathetic to aspects of this cause, we challenge the underlying mantra of 'diverse tools, shared standards' (Brady and Collier 2010). This book attends to the question of how small facts can speak to large issues from the other side of the naturalist–humanist divide. We seek not only to provide an overlapping set of tools, but also a distinct set of standards by which to conduct and judge comparative interpretive research.

This contribution is vital because interpretive social science remains widely typecast as idiographic, both among its critics *and* its practitioners. For naturalist social scientists, interpretivists – if they enter the conversation at all – are deemed to be in the business of 'mere description'. They provide rich, detailed and illuminating accounts of isolated social phenomena, but the relationship to theory building and testing is tangential at best. Insofar as naturalists seek accommodation with the humanist tradition, it is by adopting a strict division of labour in which detailed descriptive inferences are reinterpreted by social scientists seeking law-like generalisability (see Gerring 2012b). Some humanist scholars who embrace, or at least are sympathetic to, the interpretive approach, invert this condescension and wear their idiographic robe with pride (for discussion, see Bates 1997). Following Geertz (1973), these scholars provide 'thick descriptions'; that is, rich, detailed and illuminating accounts of particular social phenomena. Theoretical generalisation is seen as a fraught and fallible task (Abu-Lughod [1991] 2006; Vrasti 2008). But whether 'mere' or 'thick', whether meant as disparaging or approving, the dividing line stays the same. The common perception is that the interpretive enterprise remains rich, but context-bound, and idiographic, unable to see the wood through the trees (see Chapter 2).

We join a swelling group of interpretive scholars who are dissatisfied with this state of affairs. The group traverses diverse fields including comparative politics (for example, Fujii 2013; Wedeen 2010); organisational studies (for example, Flyvbjerg 2006); public health (for example, Greenhalgh et al. 2011); human geography (for example, Robinson 2011); international relations (for example, Pouliot 2014); and area studies (for example, Gibson-Graham 2004; Wesley-Smith and Goss 2010). We argue that the dichotomy between the naturalist pursuit of analytical clarity and generalisability and the humanist pursuit of rich idiographic detail is a false one (cf. Brady and Collier 2010; Coppedge 2012; King, Keohane and Verba 1994): interpretive researchers can and do make meaningful comparisons that speak to themes of general significance (see Adcock 2006; Bevir and Rhodes 2015, part 2). Our goal is to outline and promote this distinctly interpretive way of thinking about and doing comparative research.

There are at least four main reasons interpretivists might want to compare. The first is that comparison provides us with a better understanding of a particular case. So, we compare cases A, B and C because they help shed new and illuminating light on case D, which is the one we are interested in. Relatedly, comparison can also help us provide policy solutions – we can suggest a policy response to case D because we know what happened in cases A, B and C. Much interpretive comparison that does exist is justified on these grounds. A third rationale is that we place a particular case in a broader social context. Nothing in this book contradicts attempts to undertake these types of comparison. But our primary rationale is that we compare because it is essential to providing 'decentred' explanations of the social world. To decentre is to unpack practices as the contingent beliefs and actions of individuals as the basis for explanation, as opposed to laws and rules, correlations between social categories or deductive models. The risk of in-depth idiographic studies is that they treat context as the de facto explanation for all social and political phenomenon, rendering impossible any attempt to generate more general insights. We argue that decentred explanations can speak to general themes. But, to do so we need to rethink the nature of comparison.

We argue that the dilemmas actors experience in their everyday lives are the intellectual skeleton key that unlocks the potential of comparative interpretive research. When we ask why actors act, we create an opportunity for reflection on alternative meanings and actions, and the pros and cons of each. By reflecting *with* actors, we uncover the choices and questions they confront. By understanding how they *see* these choices, as a reflection of the webs of belief in which they are embedded, we are able to explain why actors do what they do. In Geertz's (1973: 15) classic formulation 'we begin with our own interpretations of what our informants are up to, or think they are up to, and then systematise those'. When we ask whether others experience the same dilemmas, we necessarily explore how their experience is either similar or different, unlocking the comparative dimension of this approach. By abductively moving back and forth between the meanings and beliefs of individual actors and our sensemaking of their practices, we provide an interpretation of their interpretations. The result is a decentred approach that focuses on the social construction of a practice – theirs and ours – through the ability of individuals to create, and act on, meanings.

So, this book is a call to arms for interpretivists to embrace creatively comparative work that uses the dilemmas of situated agents as its empirical starting point to develop plausible conjectures. It justifies and explains the approach. We hope that researchers across social science disciplines might find inspiration in our attempt to reassert the place of richly inter- pretive analysis in broader theory-building efforts. Readers searching for a comprehensive, step-by-step guide to conducting interpretive compa- rative research will most likely be disappointed. There is simply not space to spell out in any detail the philosophical basis of the interpretive approach nor to provide a textbook on qualitative data collection and analysis. In fact, there is no need. Existing textbooks and handbooks do this job comprehensively (see, for example, Bevir and Blakely 2018; Bevir and Rhodes 2015; Schaffer 2015; Schwartz-Shea and Yanow 2012 Yanow and Schwartz-Shea 2006; Wagenaar 2011). We focus on demonstrating, with concrete examples, the potential of a *comparative* interpretive approach. The examples come from our fieldwork and the work of scholars who have adopted a similar approach even if they would not explicitly identify it as comparative interpretive work. The argument is therefore not limited to political science but applies equally to richly qualitative research in cognate disciplines in the social sciences and humanities.

This chapter consists of five substantive sections. First, we outline our basic argument. Here, we put forward the need for a consciously and expli- citly comparative interpretive approach, and the creative benefits that such an approach can provide. Second, we provide a brief summary of the interpretive approach. Third, we seek to justify the rigour and sensitivity of a comparative interpretive orientation. Fourth, we foreshadow in greater depth the structure of the book and detail of its component chapters. Finally, we provide guidance for readers on how to use the book, and in particular on how to combine its insights with those stemming from canonical texts in the field.

The Comparative Intuition

At the heart of this book is the idea that comparing is intuitive (see Anderson 2016). People in general, and social scientists in particular, are engaged in 'constant comparison'. Comparison is what enables us to make sense of events as they unfold across time and space. We compare to identify patterns and disjuncture in the social world. We compare new experiences with old ones to help us make sense of the exotic or unfamiliar. By doing so, we sometimes see familiar settings in a new light. We also draw on comparisons to help communicate ideas and make insights interesting for a broad audience. Human beings are comparative animals.

Seen in these terms, naturalist approaches to social science discipline and restrict the comparative intuition. Here, comparison is something to be designed into the project from the beginning. The core problem – and one to which anyone with experience of detailed fieldwork can attest – is that the best-laid comparative plans can go wrong. Expected categories of comparison can melt away on closer inspection. Unexpected categories can emerge to take their place. As Gerring (2007: 149) concedes in highlighting the limits to even the most careful and robust process of case selection in naturalist research: 'Not all twists and turns on the meandering tail of truth can be expected'.

Meanwhile, humanist approaches to the social sciences tend to smother the comparative intuition. The goal is to understand and highlight the rich specificities of the context under examination. Attempts to draw out comparative themes across cases can be derided as erasing or blunting these specificities. This concern is at the heart of the radical critique of efforts to draw broader theoretical lessons from bespoke settings (see e.g. Vrasti 2008). The effect, ironically given the commitment of these humanist scholars to reflexivity, is to wish away a key part of the interpretive process. Doing so prevents analysts from reflecting on, and giving voice to, how they impose their own sense-making systems and categories on their data in order to render their fieldwork observations intelligible to others.

We argue that interpretivists who embrace the comparative intuition can overcome these limitations. Unlike the naturalist approach to disciplining this intuition, such a move can enable the analyst to explore comparative insights that emerge in the field after the development of authentic and in-depth case knowledge. Unlike the humanist approach to denying or negating this intuition, it can authentically present the world as the analyst sees and experiences it. Indeed, rather than flatten or misrepresent context, comparison in these terms becomes a vital means of both *understanding* and *conveying* context. It is only through comparison that new insights and experiences become meaningful, and we can communicate meaningfully to relevant audiences.

Embracing the comparative intuition can also help immensely in unlocking creativity. Creativity is central to all forms of social science research but little understood. Kaufman and Beghetto (2009) usefully distinguish between Big-C creativity and Pro-C creativity. Big-C creativity refers to 'the remarkable and lasting contributions made by mavericks in some domain', while Pro-C (or professional creativity) refers to 'professional creators, [who] have not reached eminent status' (and for a review of the field see Kozbelt, Beghetto and Runco 2010). Scholars in both naturalist and humanist traditions produce work of Pro-C quality, but work of Big-C quality is frustrated increasingly by the restrictive paradigms in which they work. Leading naturalists concede that, in spite of their advocacy of strict standards and rigid protocols, creativity remains an elusive but essential ingredient in good research. It enables researchers to situate their findings, to design and execute effective research programmes and, above all, to find the spark of inspiration that propels the voyage of discovery. In their naturalist bible for political science, for example, King, Keohane and Verba (1994: 14) quote Karl Popper approvingly: 'Discovery contains an "irrational element", or a "creative intuition".' Yet, in practice, any sense of creativity is all too often suppressed when writing-up findings (cf. Feyerabend 1988; Gerring 2017; Polanyi 1958). Indeed, thoughtful writers of a naturalist persuasion have acknowledged this methodological bind. For example, Collier, Brady and Seawright (2010: 197) write that naturalist procedures may 'sharply narrow their substantive research questions, thus producing studies that are less important'. They identify a conflict between 'the methodological goals of improving descriptive and causal inference' and 'the objective of studying humanly important outcomes'. Gerring (2017: 31–32) goes further when he states that 'the task of discovery is a comparatively anarchistic affair. There are no rules for finding new things' (Gerring 2017: 31).

If naturalist social science favours justification (i.e. verification and refutation) over discovery, humanist social science favours exploration and innovation. Leading proponents typically present the opportunity to be creative as one of the chief virtues, and pleasures, of this approach to social science (see most famously Geertz 1973). The core logic is to move iteratively between an inductive account of the data and a deductive reading of the relevant literature, thus leaving space for creativity to flourish. For example, Geertz's (1973: chapter 15) famous account of the Balinese cockfight starts by describing it as a vice raid – cockfighting is illegal. Next, he interprets it as a symbol of Balinese masculinity – the double entendre of cockfighting is deliberate. The next layer of meaning is cockfighting as blood sacrifice to keep demons at bay. It is followed by a discussion of gambling that casts cock fighting as a dramatisation of status concerns in the tiered status hierarchy of Balinese society; men are allegorically humiliating one another, although their status is not changed by the cockfight's outcome. Finally, he considers the cockfight as a typical spurt in Balinese life. Cockfighting is the story the Balinese tell themselves about themselves. Cockfighting is no longer a vice but a text that Geertz is reading to say something about Balinese culture. His account is both a creative and a masterly thick description of small facts speaking to large issues.

However, in practice, most authors remain narrowly channelled, bound by the focus on the specific context, which takes priority over all else. In the humanist tradition, rigour is defined as the richest, most bespoke forms of contextual knowledge. So, interpretive researchers working in the humanist tradition feel free to forge their own creative connections to broad theoretical concerns. But only if theory speaks to the specific context under examination. Breadth must be sacrificed for depth. Those who do manage to escape this trap, and speak to broader debates, risk scorn. Take James C. Scott's (1979, 1985, 1990) hugely influential trilogy on agrarian politics as an exemplar; it has been humorously categorised across graduate classrooms as 'First, peasants in Malaysia; then, peasants everywhere; finally, everyone everywhere!' (see Rabinowitz 2014).

More commonly, then, it is skilful scholars working on particular issues who have a big impact on the field. Seemingly, we cannot explain or reproduce their broader impact. Again, we confront a form of magic or alchemy by which the rich insights of humanist scholarship somehow achieve broad resonance.

The key to demystifying this alchemy, we argue, is to unlock creativity in making comparisons. We use the word 'puzzling' to describe this creative process. It refers to solving a problem or answering a question creatively (see also Adcock 2006: 62). It may involve clever guesswork or a novel experiment. We are drawn to the word for two reasons. First, it contains its own contradiction. If something is a puzzle, it means it confuses us, yet by puzzling over the confusion we attempt to make sense of it. The field – and especially the multiple fields entailed in comparative research – can throw up many puzzles we do not understand, so we puzzle over them to find their meanings. Fujii (2013), for example, is puzzled by why acts of extralethal violence (e.g. forcing victims to dance and sing before killing them, mutilation and so forth) occur. Given the risks involved, these acts defy rationalist explanations. Using cases from Vietnam, Rwanda and Malaysia, she argues that these acts can be explained by the participants' roles and activities, which contribute by producing graphic effects. This type of work operates according to a 'logic of discovery' – iterative, open-ended, evolving – as opposed to the typical social science preference for a 'logic of justification' in which invariant procedures are rigorously applied with the aim of producing generalisable and predictive results.

Following a 'logic of discovery', the second attraction is that puzzling is a process with no clear destination; we change the puzzle as we seek to resolve our confusions, often multiple times over the course of a complex comparative project. Through deep, rigorous and continuous puzzling, interpretive scholars can feel emboldened to explore and tease out comparisons that surprise and intrigue, that uncover new insights or force readers to confront familiar insights in new ways. In this way, our account of interpretive comparison can provide a new set of tools and insights to seed, exploit and channel creativity in crafting effective and affecting comparison.

Interpretation and Comparative Intuition

Interpretive research offers a distinctive approach to channelling the comparative intuition because it consciously offers interpretations of interpretations. It concentrates on meanings, beliefs and discourses, as opposed to laws and rules, correlations between social categories, or deductive models. An interpretive approach is not alone in paying attention to meanings. It is distinctive because of the extent to which it privileges meanings as ways to grasp actions. Its proponents privilege meanings because they hold, first, beliefs have a constitutive relationship to actions and, second, beliefs are inherently holistic.

For example, when other political scientists study voting behaviour using attitude surveys or models of rational action, they separate beliefs from actions to find a correlation or deductive link between the two. In contrast, an interpretive approach suggests such surveys and models cannot tell us why, say, raising one's hand should amount to voting. They do not tell us why there would be uproar if someone forced someone else to raise their hand against their will. We can explain such behaviour only if we appeal to the intersubjective beliefs that underpin the practice. We need to know voting is associated with free choice and, therefore, with a particular concept of the self. Practices could not exist if people did not have the associated beliefs. Beliefs or meanings would not make sense without the practices to which they refer.

The aim of interpretive research is to decentre: to unpack practices as the contingent beliefs and actions of individuals as we just did with our short example of voting. Decentred analysis produces detailed studies of people's beliefs and practices. It focuses our attention on everyday dilemmas. It challenges the idea that inexorable or impersonal forces drive politics, focusing instead on the relevant meanings, the beliefs and preferences of the people involved. Like a kaleidoscope, decentring produces changing patterns. We use this metaphor to allude to the way that all agents are situated within multiple, intersecting social fields (age, gender, ethnicity, profession, etc.). The classic social science approach is to make each field the subject of empirical analysis. Starting with agents rather than fields allows us to see how dilemmas recur and intersect. The effect is akin to looking through a kaleidoscope, with the same practices and processes given new meaning depending on the agent narrating it.

Not Anything Goes

In seeking to unlock the creativity of interpretive comparison, we want to be clear that we do not suggest that 'anything goes'. Underlying this scepticism is a suspicion that any attempt to bridge the particular–general divide in an interpretive approach necessarily entails a lack of rigour. We do not so much have in mind here the scepticism that might be expected from naturalist social scientists. While we will argue that such scholars might derive important insights from close engagement with our argument, we do not expect them to come all the way with us. To invert the common mantra here, we have some shared tools, but different standards. Instead, our chief target is the humanist impulse to look down on any attempt to go beyond idiography as 'airplane ethnography' (Bevir and Blakely 2018: 94); a pale, even dangerous, imitation of the real thing. We combine breadth and depth and focus our discussion on defending the rigour of comparative interpretive research against such prejudices (see Chapter 4).

Rigour in the humanist tradition depends on reflexivity. A long-standing and penetrating critique of the naturalist approach is that it airbrushes out persistent normative biases that bump up against the naturalist pursuit of objectivity. The obvious example is the Cold War biases that permeate the literature on comparative democratisation (de Volo 2015). So, contrary to the naturalist pursuit of objectivity, the humanist response embraces subjectivity, and all its associated idiosyncratic practices and interpretations (see especially Schwartz-Shea and Yanow 2012: chapter 6). Rigour stems from a deep commitment to reflexivity throughout a research project. It is reflected in a rejection of uniform procedures and universal standards and a focus on how the subjective position of the researcher shapes their practice. Such discussion typically centres on explicit reflection on the researcher's role in the *social* field of their research. It will consider such issues as their status as an insider or outsider; their normative preferences; and the disadvantages and privileges that enable or hinder access. A good example is Yanow and Schwartz-Shea's (2006) edited volume on *Interpretation and Method*, which has become something of a staple on more pluralist graduate programmes in political science and social policy. Each chapter begins with the authors' personal reflections on their own experiences and commitments, and the ways in which they shaped their research journey. The handbook illustrates the reflexivity expected of interpretive research.

This practice cannot be disentangled from debates about dominant cultural norms in academic practice, especially the long tradition of western ethnocentrism in disciplines such as Anthropology and History (Clifford and Marcus 1986). It stems in particular from the ripples of the 'Culture War' in Anthropology that began in the 1980s and dominated the 1990s. The point of reflexivity is to acknowledge the analyst's social position; to foreground the total immersion that such a research project entails; to highlight the obstacles and challenges such immersion presents; and to clear the way for a richer and more authentic representation of how the subjects of interpretive research see their world.

We take no issue with such reflexive criticism. However, the way in which it is practised can be a problem. The risk is a new form of academic chauvinism or gatekeeping in which only those with the requisite demographic background can perform the role of expert with authority. This stance denies the legitimacy of 'outsider' perspectives; for example, the criticisms levelled at Anderson for his parallels between Southeast Asia and the West (Anderson 2016: 149). Moreover, it presents only a partial view of the experiences and normative preferences that influence academic scholarship.

The researcher's position in the *social* field is one thing, but what about their position in the *academic* field? Researchers have particular sets of beliefs and normative preferences based not just on their personal histories, but also on their professional socialisation. We do not want to impugn the reputation of other scholars. In fact, we draw on examples of how professional norms, pressures and ambitions have shaped our own work throughout subsequent chapters. It is simply to recognise that research does not take place in a neutral professional context. The academy, as anyone who has spent any time in it can attest, is not short of tempting bandwagons and powerful cliques. Certain sorts of research attract rewards such as grants, prestige and impact more than others. Career prospects and legacies are at stake. What we study, how we study it and how we represent our findings can all be affected by presumptions, aspirations and doubts about how our work will be received (see especially Hay 2011).

There are important personal and professional questions underlying different comparative strategies. Why do we seek to compare, or refrain from comparing, in particular circumstances? Why do we choose particular ways to compare particular phenomena? What are we trying to achieve? Humanists in the idiographic tradition have typically refrained from answering these questions directly. In the hands of some of the most skilful practitioners, such choices are apparent. Take, for example, Lisa Wedeen's (2007) study of *qat* chewing in Yemen. Wedeen depicts the organic deliberation enabled by this cultural practice by using an implicit comparison with Habermas's (1989) account of the emerging public sphere in Parisian salons. Through carefully crafted attribution, allusion and mimicry, she develops an account that speaks to a broad audience well beyond Yemeni experts or Middle East scholars. But not all interpretive research can be so creative and artful, and not all readers are going to be equipped to appreciate such intertextual subtleties.

We seek here to provide a more straightforward approach to reflexivity. We promote a consciously and explicitly comparative interpretive approach that can bring these design, interpretive and discursive choices out into the open. By focusing on dilemmas, we follow the humanist approach in putting people at the centre of our analysis. We commit to trying to present our research participants' world as (we think) they see and feel it. But in identifying, developing and fleshing out comparisons, we must acknowledge ways in which their dilemmas are familiar or alien to us. Such puzzling will reveal how our own views and experiences skew our account of their beliefs and practices. So, the creative drawing of comparisons forces us to acknowledge how our personal experiences and biases inflect our practice. Second, by seeking to compare such dilemmas across contexts, we must be explicit about how and why we are linking our research to major theoretical themes. In doing so, we reveal something about what we are trying to achieve politically and professionally. We acknowledge our position in the academic field by putting our own normative preferences and intentions up front.

Understanding and practising reflexivity in this way opens interpretive comparative research up to scrutiny from more angles than either naturalist or humanist work typically allows. By consciously laying out the theoretical claims we seek to make through such comparison, we welcome the scrutiny of the generalists working on that theme. Our desire to make 'plausible conjectures' of general interest necessarily entails both a tight theoretical argument and much critical reflection on the broader resonance of the dilemmas at the heart of our comparative findings. Just as important, because our focus on dilemmas means we still strive to represent the research participants' world, we still welcome the scrutiny of the specialist. Central to our account of rigour is the forensic interrogation of competing narratives by both specialists and practitioners (Bevir and Rhodes 2003: 37–40). Our comparative approach *multiplies* our readership and potential critics. Our accounts of the dilemmas that actors face need to ring true with scholarly and local or practitioner audiences across all the different settings under analysis.

We do not advance the bold claim that comparative interpretive research is somehow *more* rigorous than other forms of social science. It is just to stress that it is no *less* rigorous. Naturally, such an approach entails trade-offs associated with the fossilised ideas about rigour in either naturalist or humanist traditions. For the former, our approach sacrifices stable variables for more fluid and subjective dilemmas. But the theoretical insights we derive still need to resonate more broadly, and still need to stand up to scrutiny when placed against the experiences and patterns established elsewhere in the field. For the latter, our approach sacrifices some depth of contextual knowledge for breadth of insight. But the claims we make about local contexts still need to have sufficient depth and richness to resonate with experts in these fields. They still need to be accurate, nuanced and context-ually sensitive (see also Adcock 2006: 62).

We do not abandon rigour. We just understand rigour in an older and more encompassing sense of the term: as shared canons of accuracy and precision, rigorous argument, clear presentation, respect for evidence and openness to criticism (see Collini 2012: 62). Our account underpins a vision of comparison not as a hard science, nor as an exercise in dangerous or whimsical speculation, but as a challenging craft, indeed an art form (see also Schmitter 2009). This book will give interpretive social scientists working in the humanist tradition key tools and techniques to set about this creative work. We outline a set of principles, standards and approaches for producing richly detailed comparative research that speaks directly to issues of general interest.

Structure of the Book

The heart of this book revolves around the following interrelated questions:

1. What are the principles and standards that guide comparative interpretive research?
2. What are dilemmas and why do they matter?
3. How do we design a comparative interpretive project?
4. How do we undertake comparative interpretive fieldwork?
5. How do we interpret and analyse comparative data?
6. How do we communicate the findings of comparative interpretive research?

These questions form the core chapters. We devote Chapters 3–7 to outlining and demonstrating the practice of interpretive comparative research. For every chapter, we do not offer rigid procedures or laws to follow. Instead, we offer various 'rules of thumb' that will help. Following the Oxford English Dictionary, we define 'rule of thumb' as a 'method or procedure derived from practice or experience, rather than theory or scientific knowledge; a roughly practical method'. Also, we provide examples from our own comparative work: on Westminster governments; policy advice to prime ministers and ministers in Australia, Britain, Canada and New Zealand; the everyday life of chiefs of staff to Australian prime ministers; policies on obesity in Australia and Britain; political leadership in small Pacific states; and poverty across different communities on the affluent South Coast of England. We outline every chapter below.

To be clear, although there is some theory in the first half of the book, it is not our intention to rake over old ground on the methods and the philosophy of social science. Much has already been written on this topic, and we do not feel it is necessary to rehearse the philosophical underpinnings of the interpretive approach we favour yet again (see Bevir and Rhodes 2003, 2006, 2010; Rhodes 2017). Instead, we focus on the specific interpretive theory that underpins our approach

Chapter 2 outlines briefly the difference between naturalism and humanism before providing a summary of our key concepts of decentring, situated agency and plausible conjectures. In effect, it sets the theoretical scene for the rest of the book and provides the underpinnings for comparative analysis based on the concept of dilemmas.

An important subsidiary aim of this chapter is to challenge assumptions about the means and aims of interpretive research. We confront a series of unhelpful myths – that, for example, interpretive research is 'mere description' useful only for uncovering contextual detail. Instead, we pave the way for an account of interpretivism which makes comparison not just possible, but fruitful." We set out a new set of criteria by which interpretive comparative work should be assessed and towards which interpretive comparative researchers ought to strive. We focus on accuracy, openness and aesthetics. We define accuracy as meaning the use of established standards of evidence and reason; so, we will prefer one narrative to another if it is more accurate, comprehensive and consistent. We define openness as taking criticism seriously and preferring positive speculative theories that open new avenues of comparison and make new conjectures supported by evidence. We show that not anything goes in comparative interpretive research.

Chapter 3 explains the concept of dilemmas and why we use it in preference to other ideas such as process and practice. Dilemmas underpin the logic of interpretive comparison. As currently used, however, it refers mainly to 'Big-D' dilemmas that focus on ideational clashes between traditions such as the clash between neoliberalism and state ownership. We add the notion of 'small-d' dilemmas that focus on the everyday, the routine and the mundane choices, 'court' politics and realpolitik.

We suggest that dilemmas perform a dual function that gives them this particular analytical importance. First, the dilemmas actors experience in their everyday actions and practice are the authentic manifestation of the social tensions that typically motivate social scientific inquiry, especially interpretive research. Second, though always embedded in local contexts, dilemmas recur across different settings. Our reading of Bailey's (1969: xi) comparison of De Gaulle and French presidential politics with village leadership in rural India shows that a concept like (in his case) 'rules of the game' or (in our case) 'dilemmas' can render social phenomena both interesting *and* comparable.

We suggest that empirical, comparative, interpretive social science research revolves around the process of identifying the dilemmas that actors experience, the ways they respond to them and puzzling about whether they vary according to the traditions in which they are situated. We suggest eight rules of thumb for identifying dilemmas.

The next four chapters of the book drill down into the practices of comparative interpretive research. We use our own experiences of conducting comparative interpretive research to reflect on the unique challenges and opportunities associated with this approach, and to provide clear and pragmatic guidance for those hoping to adopt it. For each chapter, we identify six to eight rules of thumb to guide the research. The four component chapters follow the widespread and stylised account of the different stages of research: design, fieldwork, analysis and writing-up. However, we emphasise throughout that this is not a linear process. Interpretive researchers always move back and forth, puzzling about and refining their project as they go, a process typically called 'abduction' (Law 2004; Schwartz-Shea and Yanow 2012; Wagenaar 2011).

Chapter 4 looks at how to design a comparative interpretive project and tackle the perennial case selection question. The problem here is one of justifying unorthodox comparison. A lot has been written on comparative case selection from a naturalist perspective, but this language is often an uncomfortable fit for interpretive projects. We argue that case selection is not something that is designed into a project from inception. For interpretive research, it changes as we go. We suggest, therefore, different strategies of case selection for different phases of a comparative interpretive project. We identify rules of thumb to guide design choices as the project or programme evolves.

Chapter 5 outlines the place of fieldwork in comparative interpretive research. Detailed qualitative fieldwork is central to most interpretive research, but practical guidance on how to navigate the field remains rooted in the idiographic tradition. The presumption is one of sustained immersion in a discrete setting. Interpretive comparison, however, necessarily requires partial immersion across multiple sites. Crucially, the researcher must be alert to the surprises and moments of epiphany that can challenge initial assumptions and open new possibilities. We seek here to develop and illustrate key 'rules of thumb' that will enable researchers to manage the challenges and maximise the opportunities.

In Chapter 6, we explain, and illustrate with examples drawn from our own work, how interpretive researchers analyse comparative data. We argue that a comparative project compounds the uncertainty, confusion and paralysis that can set in when confronted with a 'mountain' of qualitative data. We argue it is not possible to 'somehow capture' this full complexity. We outline and defend the need for a consciously impressionistic orientation to data analysis. Rather than searching for a 'Eureka!' moment that confirms or refutes a narrow theory (in naturalist or nomothetic mode) or makes sense of the whole picture (in idiographic mode), a comparative focus on dilemmas enables the use of a kaleidoscope of different analytical lenses and tools to explore complex specificness in context. We outline rules of thumb for helping along the way.

Chapter 7 looks at the craft of writing. Although we discuss the challenges of writing that confront all social scientists, we focus on the dilemmas of writing-up comparative interpretive research – dilemmas which we confront because we speak to a broader range of audiences. We focus on the dilemmas around structure, style and substance. In doing so, we highlight the importance of seeing writing as integral to the research process, not something that starts once the research is done.

In Chapter 8, we turn our methods back on our own book and ask, 'what are the dilemmas of using the approach we advocate?' It is an exercise in professional reflexivity as we reflect on the personal dilemmas that we navigated in writing this book. Also, we take a last opportunity to impress on the reader the merits of this approach by summarising the key terms of both the interpretive approach and our comparative interpretive approach. It is a short cut for those who like to skim books before reading them.

How to Use this Book

This book serves different functions for different readers and we think ought to be read in different ways by these audiences. Experienced scholars, well acquainted with the humanist–naturalist and particular–general divides, and familiar with the details of research design and practice, will be able to read it against that background. For naturalists, it is a sophisticated and grounded challenge to common presumptions about interpretive work. These scholars have been responsible for much of the most innovative and exciting work in seeking to promote the general value of case research (see Brady and Collier 2010; George and Bennett 2005; Gerring 2017; Goertz and Mahoney 2012). This flowering of ideas and strategies has served to push along sophisticated thinking in interpretive research methods (see, for example, Pouliot 2014). We hope that our attempt to tackle the issue from the other side of the divide might have a similar effect. For humanists, the book is not an indictment of rich idiographic work. We think such research remains important. It is simply an invitation to scholars in this tradition to be more open to the prospect of drawing comparison. And it is a how-to guide with detailed advice on innovative ways to tailor and augment their approach. Readers in either tradition may not be persuaded, but we hope at least they find our perspective interesting and valuable.

Those colleagues now learning the craft, still feeling their way through methodological debates and new to issues like case selection, data collection and analytical techniques, may need to approach the book rather differently. They will likely benefit from reading chapters alongside orthodox textbooks and handbooks on qualitative and interpretive inquiry. Any lack of knowledge should not stop such readers understanding what we say. It is simply that they will need those nuts and bolts also to understand and justify the range of methods entailed by a complex social science project. The book is designed to be a thought-provoking and accessible accompaniment to the established canon in qualitative and humanist social science. Our hope is to encourage newcomers (as well as old-timers) to be ambitious about the impact they can make by learning to practice the art and craft of comparison.

2 Interpretation

The theory chapter is often a problem. Readers already familiar with the approach are likely to think here we go again, raking over old ground in the philosophy of the social sciences. The converted already know this stuff by heart, and the doubting Thomas will not even glance at it. We sent a draft of the book to several friends and colleagues and received some vigorous replies. Paul 't Hart recommended we leave out the theory chapter:

I hate it that interpretivists always feel compelled to take us down that particular dull alley whenever they fart. The less the better I'd say. Just reference that stuff and get on with your core business. Avoid yet another generic, defensive and repetitive promulgation of interpretive research.

He skipped the theory chapter:

Sorry, couldn't bear reading it in detail. The level of abstraction, the juxtapositions and characterisations of epistemologies – seen it all before, over and over. Unwittingly you confirm the stereotype that interpretivists feel compelled to go first to the philosophy of science stratosphere before they say or do anything. It is precisely these grand but vacuous claims that put many people off interpretivism. Instead of talking about it in these abstract terms, just get on with it and SHOW it. Sorry for the irony and sarcasm, but you promised a methods' text on the art of comparison, so where are the fucking methods, comparison, art and craft? Please get on with talking about what you have promised your readers you would talk about: how to do comparison in interpretive research.

He has a point. But, we feel we cannot do the book without this chapter because: (1) the rationale for our approach to comparison is grounded in a particular philosophy, so the uniqueness of this book, the concepts we employ and the way we employ them, stems from our position in these admittedly esoteric debates; and (2) not all readers will be familiar with the established interpretive canon. Certainly, we would not expect PhD scholars to be as familiar with these long-standing debates as senior professors. Parts of the world also teach and value the interpretive approach differently. So, we decided to be frank. If you know interpretive theory already, and particularly interpretivism according to Bevir and Rhodes (2003, 2006, 2010), skip the chapter. If, like Paul, you are allergic to it, skip the chapter. If you have not encountered interpretive theory before, read on. We provide a short, hopefully accessible account for anyone who feels the need to get to grips with interpretivist approaches as we see and use them.

Before moving to a more abstract discussion, we start with a story from Geertz's (1980) analysis of *Negara*; of the king and court of the Balinese state to show the importance of looking through a kaleidoscope at the social construction of institutions. A kaleidoscope can shed new light on other people's worlds; we see the same places in new ways. Most people have inherited beliefs about the meaning of words like king and court. It might be Henry VIII, his six wives and the ruthless court politics of Thomas Cromwell. It might be Louis XIV of France, *le roi soleil*, the extravagances, architectural and personal, of his palace at Versailles, and his successful struggle for control over the aristocracy. But Negara turns our notions of king and court on their head.

The Balinese king and court did not sully their hands with running a country. Rather, they practised pomp and circumstance, dramatising their superiority by public rituals and ceremonies. These rituals were the state:

The whole of the Negara – court life, the traditions that organized it, the extractions that supported it, the privileges that accompanied it – was essentially directed toward defining what power was; and what power was was what kings were. . . . The driving aim of higher politics was to construct a state by . . . constructing a king. The more consummate the king, the more exemplary the centre. The more exemplary the centre, the more actual the realm. (Geertz 1980: 124)

Geertz develops the notion of the theatre state in which:

the 'real' is as imagined as the imaginary . . . [and] . . . the dramas of the theatre state . . . were . . . neither illusions nor lies, neither sleight of hand nor make believe. They were what there was. (Geertz 1980: 136)

The point of looking through a kaleidoscope is that actions can be viewed from many points. Geertz's portrait is controversial, and there are debates over the respective merits of hydraulic bureaucracy, oriental despotism and the theatre state as explanations of kingly supremacy. These debates are not our main point. For an interpretive approach, Geertz's analysis is significant because he focuses on the beliefs and actions of individuals exercising their particular reasoning in given social contexts. No other approach would focus on the importance accorded to the mythic and the symbolic and their capacity to shape what we call 'reality'.

In the rest of this chapter, we outline an approach to interpretive theory that draws on and extends Bevir and Rhodes's version. The chapter proceeds in four sections. First, we outline the traditional 'two worlds' account of interpretivism and its mainstream other in order to anticipate the problems of interpretivism. In the sections that follow, we focus on four unhelpful 'myths' associated with the interpretive approach:

1. By pursuing 'thick description', interpretivism can only elicit understanding.
2. In foregrounding actors' 'webs of meaning' interpretivism grants actors undue autonomy.
3. In uncovering 'complex specificity' interpretivism provides only idiographic description.
4. Interpretivism is inherently relativist because it gives us no reason to accept that these idiographic descriptions correspond to truth.

We argue against all four of these presumptions. We highlight a set of concepts and tools that enable interpretivists to pursue explanation, to foreground the constraints on agency and how it is exercised, and to use these insights to develop plausible conjectures of broad theoretical interest.

Naturalism and Humanism

Typically, when the discipline talks about ontological and epistemological positions, it divides itself into these two competing camps. They go by various names: naturalist and humanist, positivist and interpretivist, foundationalist and anti-foundationalist (for discussion see Bevir and Blakely 2018; Bevir and Kedar 2008). We deliberately exclude qualitative and quantitative from this list as we primarily see this as a philosophical, not methodological, debate. We can use qualitative data to verify and falsify (e.g. George and Bennett 2005) just as we can use quantitative data to explore and innovate (e.g. Stone 2016). In which case, the important distinction between the main two alternatives to studying the political world is not whether the data they use are words or numbers but rather what orientation or sensibility they bring to empirical projects.

This distinction is a narrative device. We accept that it verges on caricature and can be misleading when attempting to categorise different pieces of

Table 2.1 Orientations to political research

Orientation	Sensibility	Methods	Goal	Analytical focus	Products of analysis
Naturalism – logic of justification	*Influenced by the natural sciences (and economics)*	*Plural:* but a preference for quantitative analysis	*Generalisation and prediction*	*Isolating variables*	*Causal inference*
Humanism – logic of discovery	*Influenced by the humanities*	*Plural:* but a preference for qualitative analysis	*Thick description*	*Webs of meaning*	*Complex specificity*

work. For example, many so-called positivists are interested in conceptual ambiguity (e.g. Goertz 2006) just as many so-called interpretivists, (e.g. Schaffer 2015) are interested in conceptual precision, albeit within a well-defined context (e.g. a language group). Indeed, as Kapiszewski, Maclean and Read (2015: chapter 2) highlight, the majority of political scientists adopt eclectic approaches in their empirical work. All labels are shorthand. Whichever label we propose will irritate some readers. Naturalist and humanist are used widely and will do as well as any other for developing our argument and spelling out what is at stake.

To underscore this point, there are many varieties of interpretivism or humanism (see Bevir and Rhodes 2015: chapters 2–10), which are the subject of considerable debate (see Turnbull 2016b: 386–388; and the citations in Rhodes 2017: 227–228). Bevir and Rhodes (2003, 2006, 2010) are among the leading exponents of the approach in political science. This book builds on their theoretical position, outlined fully over several books. Here we provide a brief summary for the reader unfamiliar with the approach.

In Table 2.1 naturalism refers to the idea that 'The human sciences should strive to develop predictive and causal explanations akin to those found in the natural sciences' (Bevir and Kedar 2008: 503). Known variously as positivism, behaviouralism and modernist-empiricism in the social sciences, it holds two central beliefs:

First, a conviction that all 'knowledge' ... is capable of being expressed in terms which refer in an immediate way to some reality, or aspects of reality that can be apprehended through the senses. Second, a faith that the methods and logical form of science as epitomized in classical physics can be applied to the study of social phenomena. (Giddens 1993: 136)

Humanism, on the other hand, argues that human life differs from the rest of nature because 'human action ... is meaningful and historically contingent'. The task of the human sciences is an interpretive one in search of meaning. Moreover, the epistemology of the social sciences assumes the knower and the known are independent. Humanism considers the two inseparable, interacting and influencing one another, leading to a 'fusion of horizons'; to shared interpretations (Lincoln and Guba 1985: 28, 36–38 and Table 1.1; and for thoroughgoing philosophical critiques of naturalism in the social sciences see: MacIntyre 2007; Rorty 1980; Taylor 2010 [1985]; Winch 2002; Wittgenstein (2009) [1953]).

These orientations, overdrawn as they are, entail at least four dichotomies. We contrast the naturalist focus on generalisability, isolating variables, causal inferences and refutation with the interpretive emphasis on 'thick description', 'webs of meaning', 'complex specificity' and intersubjective objectivity. We argue that this latter approach does not lead to a narrow idiographic approach or 'mere description'.

Decentring

The most obvious misconception about the interpretive approach is that it aims only to understand actions and practices, not explain them. A distinction is drawn between the nomothetic search for explanatory laws of the social sciences and idiographic understanding of the interpretive sciences. We join a growing chorus of scholars who push back against this assertion that descriptive work cannot tell a causal story (see also Gerring 2012b, 2017; Wedeen 2009). We concede that when using an interpretive logic of discovery, the causal story is typically told in a different way to the more 'mechanistic' account of causation favoured by scholars working from a logic of justification. Still, interpretivists have a clear if different notion of causation. Table 2.2 summarises their meanings of causation.

For political scientists working in a naturalist tradition, the aim of research is a formal explanation in which the effect of atomised political reality A on atomised political reality B can be observed, measured and a general law formulated. Their view of causation is modelled on the natural sciences. It is a mechanistic view of the universe. Central to this approach is ascribing causal power to fixed variables such as institutional settings or demographic characteristics.

Our interpretive logic of discovery rejects this view of the universe. We are sceptical of the idea that the laws of nature apply to the social world of

Table 2.2 Decentred research

Goal of interpretive research	Assumed implication	Our account
Thick description: The researcher writes his or her interpretation of the subject's interpretation of what the subject is up to (adapted from Geertz 1973: 9).	*Mere description:* Interpretive research is orientated to rich understanding of contextual detail, but cannot explain why social or political phenomena occur.	*Decentring:* We unpack the contingent beliefs and actions of individuals, challenging the idea that inexorable or impersonal forces drive politics. We assume people act for reasons and we aim to uncover those reasons to explain their actions.

human affairs. Instead, we seek to provide a holistic understanding of how and why agents act on beliefs that are situated within webs of belief, discourse or traditions (see Bevir and Rhodes 2003; Schwartz-Shea and Yanow 2012; Wagenaar 2011). We favour 'thick description' or complex specificity in context (Geertz 1973: chapter 1; Wolcott 1995).

Thick descriptions are not 'mere description' (see also Gerring 2012b). Rather, they represent a shift of *topos* from structures to beliefs; to meanings in action. A core premise common to interpretive approaches is that we cannot read off people's beliefs and preferences from objective facts about them such as their social class, race or institutional position. Thick descriptions embody a distinctive form of explanation, which Bevir (1999: 304–306) refers to as narrative. Some care is necessary because the term narrative has become a ubiquitous term in the twenty-first century. It comes in many guises; for example, auto-ethnography, life history, oral history, memoirs and storytelling (see Czarniawska 2004 for a survey of narratives in the social sciences). Here, we use narrative as a form of explanation.

For Bevir (1999: chapters 4 and 7) a narrative unpacks the disparate and contingent beliefs and practices of individuals through which they construct their world to identify the recurrent patterns of actions and related beliefs. The resulting narrative is not just a chronological story. Narratives explain actions by specifying the beliefs and desires that caused the actions and practices. People act for reasons, conscious and unconscious, and these reasons explain their actions.

In short, the interpretive approach is about explanation, not understanding. The natural and interpretive sciences use different concepts of causation, and the interpretive version of explanation differs from that often found among political scientists. Narratives are the way the interpretive approach explains actions and practices.

Situated Agency

An interpretive approach shifts analysis away from institutions, functions and roles to the actions and practices of webs of actors. To understand actions and practices, we need to grasp the relevant meanings; the beliefs and preferences of the people involved. Central to this task is unpacking the 'webs of meaning' that people spin for themselves. It focuses on the social construction of a practice through the ability of individuals to create, and act on, meanings. Individuals are situated in webs of beliefs handed down as traditions and these beliefs and associated practices are changed by the dilemmas people confront. A common criticism of the humanist approach is that interpretivists accord too much importance to agency and not enough to structure. The complaint is that interpretivists imagine actors performing on a clean slate so they have the autonomy to reimagine material obstacles and institutional boundaries, like King Canute holding back the tide, and develop their own idiosyncratic tale. This misunderstanding conflates agency with autonomy.

At the heart of decentred analysis is the notion of *situated agents*: that is, individuals using local reasoning consciously and subconsciously to reflect on and modify their contingent heritage. Table 2.3 summarises the idea of situated agency.

The situated agency of participants allows them to make choices about whether to retain or reshape beliefs and practices. Such agency is creative, and not fixed by rules. For example, situated agents interpret the inherited conventions and practices of (say) Congress or the House of Lords, and can vary them. This statement does not imply that all people are heroic individuals who either preserve or have great impact on the historical direction of a practice. It implies only that they have the capacity to adapt their inheritance and act in novel ways. When they do, they are unlikely to alter significantly any practice unless others also adjust their beliefs and actions. Even then, the changes in practice may not correspond to their initial intentions. A practice is a set of actions that display a pattern that can remain relatively stable across time. Such notions as institution and structure can be used as a metaphor for the way actions coalesce into stable practices. We avoid this metaphor because all too often it has a bewitching effect, leading people to

Table 2.3 Situated agency

Focus of interpretive analysis	Assumed implication	Our account
Webs of meaning: An interpretive approach focuses analytical attention on the webs of significance that people spin for themselves.	*Clean slate:* Interpretive research emphasises agency, not structure.	*Situated agency:* We see individuals as situated in wider webs of beliefs and traditions that shape their beliefs. Yet they remain agents because they make choices in response to *traditions, beliefs* and *dilemmas.*
		Beliefs are the interpretations of individuals of their world and their surroundings.
		Traditions form the background of ideas in which agents find themselves.
		A *dilemma* is an idea that stands in contradiction to other beliefs, posing a question for actors. Dilemmas are resolved by accommodating the new belief in the present web of beliefs or replacing old beliefs with new beliefs.

treat institutions or structures as real, reified entities (and for an illustration and discussion of the practices of the House of Lords, see Crewe 2005).

In sum, the way actors exercise agency is not unlimited, but situated within 'webs of meaning' – it is shaped by the beliefs, traditions and dilemmas they inherit and encounter.

Beliefs are the basic unit of analysis in interpretive research. They provide actors with interpretations of their surroundings. Beliefs do not emerge in a vacuum, though. They are part of a shared social inheritance and construction. Actors do not operate on a *clean slate*. In many naturalist accounts, institutions are said to have a concrete, fixed form; that is, they have operating rules or procedures that govern the actions of the individuals. It leads political scientists to downplay the effects of contingency, internal conflict and the several contending constructions of how things work. If we think of institutions in this way, we do not interpret what institutions mean to people. Rather, we assume the allegedly objective rules that prescribe or cause behaviour. There are two problems with this assumption. First, people not only wilfully choose to disobey a rule, but also, they subvert, ignore, avoid and redefine them. Second, we cannot read off peoples' beliefs and desires from their social location. Rules are always open to interpretation. It is not just a question of literal meaning but also a question of to whom the rule applies, and applying the rule in any given situation. As Law (1994: 263) observes, outsiders studying an organisation 'are no more able to offer a single and coherent account of the way in which it orders itself' than its managers. Therefore, as interpretivists, we search for multiple accounts because, when we include cultural factors or beliefs, then rules do not fix such meanings or the actions of its members. Instead, we ask how beliefs and actions are created and recreated to reproduce and modify institutions constantly. If we understand an institution in this way, it poses the question of whether an institutional approach remains, in any significant sense, institutional. We no longer cast explanations as if behaviour was the result of rules but as the multiple, diverse ways in which people understand, react to, interpret and reinterpret rules. In sum, we treat institutions as embedded beliefs and practices, and stress that political science is an interpretive discipline focused on the beliefs and actions of the relevant actors.

The concept of *tradition* explains why people come to believe what they do. People understand their experiences using theories they have inherited. This social heritage is the necessary, ever-evolving background to the beliefs people adopt and the actions they perform. So, a tradition is a set of understandings someone receives during a continuing, even at times episodic, socialisation. Although tradition is unavoidable, it is only a starting point, not something that determines later actions. Traditions are an unavoidable presence in everything people do, but they are mainly a first influence on people.

The potential for agency makes tradition a more satisfactory concept than rival terms such as structure, paradigm and episteme. These latter ideas suggest the presence of a social force that determines or limits the beliefs and actions of individuals. Tradition, in contrast, suggests that a social heritage comes to individuals who, through their agency, can modify this heritage even as they pass it on to others. Individuals use local reasoning consciously and subconsciously to reflect on and modify their contingent heritage (Bevir and Rhodes 2006: 4–5 and 7–9).

A *dilemma* arises for an individual or institution when a new idea stands in opposition to existing beliefs or practices and forces a reconsideration of these existing beliefs and associated tradition. Dilemma provides a way of understanding the role of individual agency in developing traditions. Whenever someone adopts a new belief or action they have to adjust their existing beliefs and practices to make way for the newcomer. To accept a new belief is to pose a dilemma that asks questions of existing traditions.

In practice, most interpretive research has focused on the 'webs of belief' that give rise to and inform dilemmas, and focused on unpacking these traditions in rich detail (for example, Bevir and Rhodes 2006). In this version, traditions can appear as context specific, hewn from rich local knowledge in ways that seemingly mitigate the prospect of comparison. But the dilemmas of daily practice that emerge from these divergent local traditions can share surprising and fruitful affinities. Examples include how the poor seek advantage (Scott 1985); whether citizen activists work with or against the establishment (Newman and Clarke 2009); and when actors choose to obey or ignore a rule (Maynard-Moody and Musheno 2003; Zacka 2017). Different actors across different contexts can face remarkably similar dilemmas in their daily practice. We expand on this claim in Chapter 3.

Plausible Conjectures

A central tenet of the interpretive orientation is that human action is historically contingent. It is:

Characterized by ineluctable contingencies, temporal fluidity and contextual specificity. Hence we cannot explain social phenomena adequately if we fail fully to take into account both their inherent flux and their concrete links to specific contexts. (Bevir and Kedar 2008: 506)

The commitment to 'complex specificness' means that mainstream political scientists often write off the value of interpretive research as idiographic. Critics claim that it is not possible to deduce laws and predict outcomes from fieldwork; that is, it is not possible to generalise. Of course, researchers can and do make general statements from a case. It is no great leap of the imagination to move from studying a retail outlet on our University campus in Southampton, UK, to sweat shops in Asia, to the glamorous world of models and designers in Paris, and to the global distribution networks of corporations. What interpretivists cannot do based on this data is make generalisations and propound laws that predict the nature of this distribution. The main reason, as Schwartz-Shea and Yanow (2012: 26–34) suggest, is that the deductive logic of inquiry so common in political science is not relevant to interpretive research. They argue that the logic of abduction is better suited.

Abductive reasoning is a:

puzzling out process [in which] the researcher tacks continually, constantly, back and forth in an iterative-recursive fashion between what is puzzling and possible explanations for it. (Schwartz-Shea and Yanow 2012: 27)

Table 2.4 Plausible conjectures

Product of interpretive analysis	Assumed implication	Our account
Complex specificity: Interpretive analysis foregrounds both the inherent flux of social and political phenomena and their concrete links to specific contexts.	*Idiographic:* Interpretive research reduces all explanation to contextual factors from which it is impossible to generalise.	*Plausible conjectures:* We can develop general statements which are plausible because they rest on good reasons and the reasons are good because they are inferred from relevant information. We use *abductive reasoning* to make these conjectures – that is, we move between the literature and emergent findings to discern patterns of broader analytical interest.

A surprise or a puzzle occurs when 'there is a misfit between experience and expectations'. The researcher is 'grappling with the process of sensemaking; of coming up with an interpretation that makes sense of the surprise'. The researcher is on an 'interpretive dance' as one discovery leads to another. If deduction reasons from its premises, and induction from its facts, then abduction reasons from its puzzle. The researcher does not deduce law-like generalisations but infers the best explanation for the puzzle. So, the interpretive researcher does not ask if the findings are generalisable but whether 'it works in context' (paraphrased from Schwartz-Shea and Yanow 2012: 46–49).

One aim of interpretive research is to explore complex specificity in context, not generalisations. It seeks to raise new questions by 'shaking the bag'. A second aim is edification from finding 'new, better, more interesting, more fruitful ways of speaking about' politics and government (Rorty 1980: 360). Interpretive research provides detailed studies of social and political dramas. It does not seek to make statistical generalisations and produce 'laws', but it does make general statements. We prefer 'plausible conjectures', because the phrase communicates the provisional nature of knowledge (see Table 2.4).

Plausible conjectures are to interpretive research what generalisations are to naturalist research. They are general statements that are plausible because they rest on good reasons, and the reasons are good because they are inferred from relevant information (Boudon 1993).

The aim is for 'small facts to speak to large issues' (Geertz 1973: 23). In a similar vein, Burawoy (1998: 5) suggests the task is to extract 'the general from the unique, to move from the "micro" to the "macro"'. We believe that such research can produce broadly resonant findings but the argument we extend here is that comparative interpretive research is especially well suited to uncovering and delivering plausible conjectures that speak to large issues. In seeking out similarities and discrepancies in the dilemmas different actors face, and parsing out the family resemblances across the different contexts, comparative interpretive researchers already have their eye trained on issues of broader theoretical significance.

Take, for example, Corbett's (2015a) work on politicians in the Pacific Islands. He was determined not to follow the dominant idiographic tradition of anthropology and area studies by treating each country or region as bespoke and unique. Instead, he searched for similarities in experience across them, and this search led him to uncover a series of common dilemmas. He showed how politicians sought to win elections by simultaneously appearing 'of' and 'apart' from their constituents; how holding office made them feel simultaneously powerful and powerless; and how they attempted to stay true to their principles while compromising to get things done. These common resemblances not only revealed new insights into Pacific politics, but they further enabled him to make plausible conjectures about the paradoxes and tensions inherent in practising democratic leadership more generally.

Plausible conjectures enable interpretivists to move from the empirical study of complex specificity in context to general analytical topics and questions. They are an intellectual shortcut that can help us better understand the topic at hand. They are the map that allows us to see the wood through the trees. They are not law-like or predictive, as their meaning and function is always open to revision and reconsideration. They are 'not about truth or falseness, but about discovery, finding new ideas' (Abbott 2004: 161; cf. Wagenaar 2011: 241–244). However, they are also analytically parsimonious and theoretically orientated, not 'mere description' (Gerring 2012b). Indeed, the important point to emphasise here is that interpretive researchers both start and end their research projects with plausible conjectures. We cannot approach an academic field or empirical question without a set of hunches about what we think is going on and why it might be interesting. The data we collect allow us to dispense with some and refine others. We then write up these findings so others can puzzle about the topic with us. In this sense, plausible conjectures function much like a hypothesis in naturalist research. The key difference is that there is no end, real or imagined, at which a plausible conjecture becomes a generalisable law with predictive qualities. Empirical work simply renders a conjecture more or less plausible.

Take a classic comparative politics topic like democratisation theory which, for example, already functions as a source of plausible conjectures. We think democratisation is likely to thrive in wealthier countries, with homogeneous populations, consensual institutions and strongly institution-alised parties (Haggard and Kaufman 2016). The point is not that these correlations can be discredited – which they can – or that there are deviant or outlier cases – which there are – but that they are analytical shortcuts that prompt discussion and debate. They provide the intellectual scaffolding on which to build the field. The plausible conjectures do not need to reflect or be present in every case. Rather, they represent a good place to begin an inquiry about the transition and consolidation of a regime. When we teach the subject, they are where we start. Moreover, when actors involved in promoting democracy or regime change are confronted with choices about how to approach a transition, they draw on these plausible conjectures. They compare their circumstances with those who have faced something similar. So, for example, plausible conjectures about how democracy works in deeply divided societies have informed the choices of agents seeking to build democratic regimes in such societies (e.g. Lijphart 1985). The results have been mixed. For example, consociational institutions have not always led to regime consolidation in deeply divided societies because they are plausible conjectures only. They do not predict an outcome, but simply provide an intellectual shortcut that can help agents resolve the dilemmas they confront. They provide an important initial step in systematically working through an issue, problem or puzzle. To borrow from a pioneer of humanistic, comparative political science, James C. Scott (2013), they are 'fun to think with'. But they are never mistaken for the 'real' thing.

Intersubjective Objectivity

All social scientists confront epistemological issues about how to evaluate narratives, models, correlations and typologies. Many positivist political scientists imply that we can justify claims to truth using logics of vindication or refutation (Carnap 1937; Popper 1959; Ricci 1984). Logics of vindication would tell us how to decide whether a statement is true. Logics of refutation would tell us how to decide whether a statement is false. Advocates of verification argue that we can decode all reasonable theories into a series of observational statements, and we can determine if these are true because they refer to pure perceptions. They conclude that a theory is true if it consists of observational statements that are true. Or it is more or less probably true according to the nature and number of observational statements in accord with it.

Advocates of refutation deny that positive observations can prove a theory true no matter how many facts we collect. They defend an ideal of refutation, arguing the objective status of theories derives from our ability to make observations that show other statements to be false. Both logics ground objectivity or truth in confrontations with basic facts. All logics of vindication and refutation believe that we can confront accounts of the world with basic facts in a test to prove them to be true or false. Their proponents typically defend the idea of basic facts by arguing that we have pure experiences of the external world. They disagree about whether the pure experiences that decide issues of truth are the particular experiences of individuals or the intersubjective experiences of a community. But they almost always defend some version of pure experience as the grounds of their logics of vindication or refutation.

An interpretive approach moves beyond vindication and refutation by drawing on its holistic analysis of meaning. Philosophical holism implies, in contrast to naturalist approaches, that we do not have pure experiences. Because meanings are holistic, experiences always embody prior theories. Therefore, we cannot determine whether an individual statement is true or false because any such conclusion has to take for granted various theoretical assumptions embodied in our experiences. An interpretive approach typically adopts a holism that implies all knowledge might be mistaken. However, to reject the idea of certainty is not necessarily to adopt a relativist position. Proponents of an interpretive approach repudiate relativism. They define objectivity as evaluation by the forensic interrogation of rival stories using reasonable criteria (and see Table 2.5; Bevir 1999: chapter 3; Bevir and Rhodes 2003: 37–40; Rhodes 2017: 30–33 and 100–102).

What are the reasonable knowledge criteria? In tune with our stress on creativity, we argue for including aesthetic criteria when evaluating comparative interpretive research. We endorse John Van Maanen's (1988: 34) call to 'be evocative in addition to being factual and truthful'. There are many other suggestions up for debate. For example, Roberts (2002: 6 and 37–40) suggests the relevant criteria include 'adequacy, aesthetic finality, accessibility, authenticity, credibility, explanatory power, persuasiveness, coherence, plausibility, trustworthiness, epistemological validity and verisimilitude' (see also Ellis 2004; Richardson 2000; Schwartz-Shea and Yanow 2012:

Table 2.5 Intersubjective objectivity

Product of interpretive analysis	Assumed implication	Our account
Narratives: Narratives explain people's actions by specifying the beliefs and desires that caused their actions and practices.	*Relativism:* There is no universal 'truth'. There are many 'truths' each specific to its historical and social context. Therefore, there are no absolute criteria for determining which narrative corresponds to truth.	*Intersubjective objectivity:* Objective knowledge arises from the forensic interrogation of the rival explanatory narratives of the academic community, practitioners and citizens. Such encounters follow the provisional rules of intellectual honesty such as established standards of evidence and reason such as shared canons of accuracy and precision, rigorous argument, clear presentation, respect for evidence and openness to criticism.

91–114; Yanow 2006). In these several endeavours, aesthetic and other criteria associated with writing fiction are prominent (and see Chapter 7). However, our main argument is that objectivity arises from using agreed facts to criticise and compare rival interpretations.

A fact is a piece of evidence that nearly everyone in the given community would accept as true. This definition of a fact follows from recognition of the role of theory in observation. Because theory is integral to observation, we cannot describe a fact as a statement of how things are. Observation and description entail categorisation. All facts come with points of view, so they are not certain truths. Objectivity arises from using agreed facts to compare and criticise rival narratives. Criticism plays a pivotal role in such an evaluation. Critics of a narrative can point to facts that its proponents have not considered. They can highlight what they take to be facts that contradict that narrative. In short, a narrative must meet tests set by its critics. Proponents of an interpretive approach defend objective knowledge as comparison between rival narratives.

This notion of objectivity raises the question of what criteria decide between rival stories. As we do throughout the book, we propose rules of thumb that treat objective behaviour as intellectual honesty in responding to criticism. The first rule is that objective behaviour requires taking criticism seriously. If people do not take criticism seriously, we will consider them biased. The second rule is that objective behaviour presupposes a preference for established standards of evidence and reason. It also assumes that challenges to settled standards should rest on impersonal and consistent criteria of evidence and reason. The third rule is that objective behaviour implies a preference for positive, speculative responses that produce exciting new stories, not ones that merely block-off criticism of existing stories. We should try to adjust our narratives in ways that extend their range and vigour.

This account of intellectual honesty gives us the criteria for comparing stories. Because we should respect set standards of evidence and reason, we will prefer narratives that are accurate, comprehensive and consistent. Our standards of evidence require us to try to support our narratives with clearly identified facts. An accurate narrative fits the facts supporting it closely. A comprehensive narrative fits many facts with few outstanding exceptions. Similarly, our standards of reasoning require us to endeavour to make our narratives clear and coherent. A consistent web of narratives holds together without going against principles of logic. Because we should favour positive speculative responses, we will prefer narratives that are progressive, fruitful and open.

The political science community's continuing forensic debates define and redefine the criteria by which we judge the knowledge claims of individual members of that community. It is not self-referential because the knowledge claims can be 'reconfirmed' by encounters with practitioners and citizens. Therefore, we translate abstract concepts into conversations in fieldwork. These encounters and their conversations produce data that we interpret to produce narratives which are then judged by evolving knowledge criteria of the relevant scholarly community. It is an iterative process. The explanations embedded in narratives are subjected to academic judgements; concepts are redefined; and again translated for new encounters and conversations in the field. In Chapter 6, we discuss the co-production of texts with practitioners. In Chapter 7, we discuss the translation of concepts for different audiences.

Proponents of an interpretive approach can defend accounts of objective knowledge as a comparison of rival narratives. Positivist political scientists might reject such an epistemology as relativist because it gives us no reason to assume the narratives that we select as objective will correspond to truth. They might argue that, even if we agree on the facts and we have criteria for comparing narratives, we still cannot declare any narrative to be true. After all, facts might be widely accepted without being true. We agree that our epistemology does not allow us to assign truth, understood as certainty, to objective knowledge. In our view, however, that is not a problem. It merely restates what should be commonplace – all knowledge is provisional.

In short, interpretive approaches are different and cannot approximate to a Popperian logic of refutation (Dowding 2016), nor should they even try. But they do need to be explicit about the criteria for comparing narratives. We have been explicit about our notion of intersubjective objectivity.

Conclusion

Our aim in this chapter has been to outline briefly an account of interpretive theory for newcomers to the approach. Interpretivists do not just seek to describe in rich detail – they seek to explain, albeit in a different, more holistic form than the naturalist approach that predominates in social science. Interpretivists do not imagine actors performing on a clean slate – they have a sophisticated account of situated agency in which actors are influenced by the beliefs, traditions and dilemmas they inherit and encounter. Interpretivists do not need to eschew claims to broader theoretical insight. While they might reject the prospect of law-like generalisability and predictability, they can certainly offer plausible conjectures which can travel across categories and contexts. Moreover, interpretivists are not relativists – objective knowledge arises from the forensic interrogation of the rival explanatory narratives of the academic community, practitioners and citizens.

This conceptual background provides the platform for our contention that interpretive research can speak beyond its idiographic boundaries. We think in-depth case studies can provide plausible conjectures, and much of our own work seeks to do just that. However, more crucially for the purposes of this book, our interpretivist account begins to sketch out a coherent logic for comparison. We have foreshadowed in this chapter the central role that dilemmas can play in enabling and underpinning comparative interpretive research. Our attention turns now to a fuller account of what dilemmas are, why they enable comparison, and how we can go about identifying and using them in comparative interpretive research.

3　Dilemmas

We have argued that an analytical focus on dilemmas is key to our approach. But what are dilemmas? How does this analytical focus enable comparison? Most importantly, how do we identify and explore dilemmas in practice? This chapter is devoted to answering these questions. Rather than test the reader's patience further with abstract theory, we attempt to answer these questions in a more practical and colourful manner. We draw on our own recent research. Our aim is to *show*, rather than tell. So, we begin the chapter with two vignettes. One is about Edna, a widow in her 50s struggling on a low income on the affluent South Coast of England. The other is about Tony, a politician from a remote Pacific Island. The vignettes reveal that these two different actors, in their own different contexts, share a remarkably similar dilemma in their everyday life and work: whether to catch the bus (or boat). The surprising affinities in the central dilemma they share open up exciting possibilities for comparison that traditional approaches to social science would preclude.

To manage expectations before we start, we clarify that we do not have space here to see these possibilities through – that more complete project will have to wait. Our aim is simply to illustrate in brief what a focus on dilemmas entails and how it can deliver on the comparative potential of interpretive research. The remainder of the chapter draws inspiration from these vignettes, and the research underpinning them, to develop key 'rules of thumb' for identifying and exploring dilemmas in practice.

The Village Bus

I'm 20 minutes early for our scheduled interview but in no mood to kill time. The desolate social housing estate, in a rural village on the Isle of Wight (IoW), offers no shelter from the driving November drizzle. So, I buzz for Edna who seems not at all perturbed by my early arrival. She bounds down the corridor with a big smile a few seconds later to fetch me, and off we go upstairs to her cosy flat.

'How did you get here?' she asks by way of introductory small talk.

'The No. 6 bus' – the only public transport linking the estate to one of the Island's town centres at least five miles away.

'That fuckin' thing! It's a miracle you arrived at all!'

Edna is familiar, funny, relaxed. She makes me a welcome cup of tea as she launches into a sardonic tirade about public transport on the Island. She explains that she is a widow in her 50s and her late husband used to drive her everywhere. Getting used to the bus 'service' after his passing some years ago has been something of a shock.

The dilemma at the centre of her daily routine, then, is whether to bother catching the bus. It represents an exorbitant expense on her meagre budget, with prices set to maximise revenue from the island's visiting summer tourists at the expense of regular local users; 'They only decide to put in a bus route because of the DFLs!' [DFL stands for Down-from-London, a derogatory term used for tourists and retirees new to the IoW].

But more than that, using the bus service means contorting all aspects of life to the rigid, threadbare timetable. It is completely impractical if she needs to work irregular hours, attend to the uncertain schedule of appointments with the public services she requires, or even do something as mundane as the weekly shopping:

EDNA: *The village is so expensive. It's actually cheaper in [the supermarket in the nearest town] and their food is better quality. But it's a lot harder now because of the buses. There is one bus that gets you there and then you've got a 40-minute window to go shopping. So most people who are on that bus are, like ... [mimes frantic shopping]*

JB: *So it's like a game show to finish your shopping?*

EDNA: *Yeah, so you run around, get your shopping and get the bus back 40 minutes later.*

Eschewing the inconveniences and indignities of the bus service, though, means barely scraping by. Edna's primary source of employment is the local pub – the steady stream of work in summer turning to a bare trickle in winter. But the pub is not a comfortable walking distance from the estate, certainly not at her age in her health. And her top-up benefit is constantly at risk because she can't always attend mandatory appointments in the nearest town centre, as required by the UK government's austere new approach to welfare. It also leaves her little choice but to shop at the expensive local store, which caters to tourists and retirees (and, as such, is an enormous source of resentment for most residents on the estate). So, to make ends meet, she has to call on favours from friends and neighbours – borrowing petty cash, doing odd jobs or cadging a lift to the pub for work.

Edna is regularly in arrears on her rent. Her saving grace is that this is the only social housing estate in the whole region with capacity it cannot fill. I'm told by Edna – and many other residents besides – that most of the families and younger people balloted here cannot tolerate the isolation, and instantly go back on the housing list in search of a place in one of the IoW's towns. Nevertheless, Edna remains under constant threat of eviction and at the sharp end of official censure. She has no disposable income to speak of. She is increasingly house bound.

She surmises with a glint of gallows' humour: 'This isn't living. It's just existing.'

Edna was happy to make another brew and keep chatting, but I had to be on my way. She instantly understood why. The last bus was due in 10 minutes, and if I missed it, I would be stuck on the estate overnight.

The Island Boat

It is late, but the bar was still open. I had been trying to find an opportunity to talk with an MP from a remote island in the central Pacific, now sitting opposite, for some time. Tony had been avoiding me. It turned out he was self-conscious about his English, but now he had had a bit to drink. His constituency, a small atoll thousands of miles from the capital, is home to around 2000 people. The population is falling. A cruise liner that used to stop off on its way to and from Hawaii doesn't come anymore. Now, the main connection between the atoll and the rest of the world is a supply ship that comes through 2–3 times a year. It is one of the smallest and remotest constituencies in the world. I wanted to know what it was like to represent it.

The bar was a long way from home for both of us. We had come for a meeting of Pacific leaders in Korror, Palau. He had to be there but was worried about how long he had been away from his constituency. The shipping schedule was irregular. The election was coming, and he didn't know if he was going to make it back in time to campaign. He was in a bind. The key concern of his constituents was that they had enough money to send their children to school and to buy rice and corned beef. But since the cruise ship stopped coming, opportunities to earn cash were rare. Part of his job as an MP was to bring economic development to the island. This meant he had to spend a lot of his time working in the capital trying to win funds. But, the more he was away, the more opportunity he provided for his political opponents to undermine him back home. Because elections in small island states are highly personalised, with political parties playing a relatively minor role, incumbent turnover is high. To keep his constituents onside and win another term he would have to put his own money in their pockets. He did not know if he would have enough.

The dilemma was a familiar one. Only a few days prior I had interviewed a congressman from a different Pacific state who also represented a remote island constituency:

The most common problem is transportation. I've been able to raise money to buy a boat. But it's not enough ... We used to have a state vessel. But I convinced the governor to sell it because that vessel was so expensive to maintain. And the fuel from here to my island and back? You won't believe it. It's $15,000! ... So, the problem is we are losing money big time. We don't have that money.

It turned out the main reason he had agreed to the interview was that he was trying to buy a sailing boat that could do the job instead. He was hoping I might be able to help. He didn't like being a politician. He felt that the demands of his constituents were too much and it was impacting his health:

To be honest I don't like it. It is a boring job. It has a lot of kiss ass lobbying things that I never imagined that I would do in my life. I didn't realise that I had to beg, that I had to give up things ... because it is a give and take situation, it is compromise, you know. It is ugly. I hate it. If you ask me the truth, politics is ugly, and please don't ever get into politics. (Corbett 2015a: 100)

What Are Dilemmas?

The first thing these vignettes can help us unpack is precisely what we mean by dilemma and what dilemmas look like in practice. In the previous chapter, we introduced the notion of dilemma as applied in the interpretive theory developed by Bevir and Rhodes. In this account, dilemmas arise:

... when a new idea stands in opposition to existing beliefs or practices and so forces a reconsideration of the existing beliefs and associated traditions. (Bevir and Rhodes 2003: 36)

The temptation – and the 'tradition' in interpretive research which has followed this approach, including some of our own (see e.g. Bevir and Rhodes 2006; Corbett 2017) – is to place emphasis on what we call Big-D dilemmas. These are reminiscent of what philosophers call 'moral dilemmas' that arise when actors are forced to make a choice between morally incompatible actions (see Dasandi and Erez 2017). They represent a disjuncture brought about by clashing traditions, as actors wrestle with radical new ideas or a rapidly changing context.

Certainly, the reflective narratives that actors tell to make sense of these dilemmas can make for a rich seam of interpretive insight. A good example is Rhodes et al.'s *Comparing Westminster* (Rhodes, Wanna and Weller 2009: 27–29). The book focuses on the key institutions of government – prime minister, ministers, public service and parliament in Australia, Britain, Canada and New Zealand – and revolves around the 'dilemmas that push [elites] to reconsider their beliefs and the intellectual tradition that informs those beliefs'. It describes the traditions underpinning those institutions – the Royal prerogative, responsible government, constitutional bureaucracy and representative government. It identifies the dilemmas confronting those institutions and their traditions – centralisation vs. decentralisation, party government vs. ministerial responsibility; professionalisation vs. politicisation; and elitism vs. participation. The book explores how elite actors reshaped their traditions in response to the dilemmas in each country. In doing so, it traces the evolution of the Westminster system of government by showing how elite actors created divergent responses to shared dilemmas.

An emphasis on Big-D dilemmas holds obvious interest and appeal. These dilemmas are often exciting and dramatic. But they are also rare in, or distant from, the everyday experience of actors. Indeed, Big-D dilemmas are not invoked directly in Edna's and Tony's stories at all. Instead, Edna's and Tony's stories open our eyes to a different sort of dilemma that shapes actors' experiences and perceptions in more mundane and pervasive ways: the small-d dilemmas of everyday practice. They are the everyday choices that these actors make in their work and life: whether to catch the bus, or whether to take formal employment or work 'under the table'; whether to chance the inconsistent boat schedule, or whether to spend finite time and resources responding to constituent needs or promoting policy priorities from afar. They shed light on the alternative responses of different actors to common problems.

These small-d dilemmas might be informed by (competing) traditions, but they are never experienced, and seldom reflected on, in such abstract terms. Recent attempts to do so by interpretivists tend to focus either on practices (Pouliot 2016) or processes (Simmons and Smith 2017). Practices, in this sense, are 'meaningful patterns of social action' which emerge and recur in everyday

Table 3.1 Big-D and small-d dilemmas

	Empirical focus	Conceptualization of change
Big-D dilemma	Human actors and the ways they co-produce traditions	Change occurs when new ideas alter established traditions
Small-d dilemma	Human actors, court politics and everyday practices	Change occurs within established traditions in response to everyday practices

interaction (Pouliot 2014: xx; see also Sullivan 2016; Wagenaar 2012). Processes, on the other hand, are a broader way of comprehending the complex dynamics which unfold in the field. Simmons and Smith (2017: 128) explain:

Where political scientists typically compare similar or dissimilar outcomes, ethnographically oriented comparison highlights political processes – that is, the dynamics and practices that shape political life – as the proverbial outcome of interest.

There are considerable affinities between these approaches and our own. Most obviously, the impetus behind both is an effort to provide a language which enables interpretivists to make comparative claims of broad theoretical relevance. But we maintain that the main value of focusing on practices and/or processes is the ability to use them as a vehicle to uncover dilemmas. For example, in his study of international conferences Pouliot (2016) observes and makes sense of the 'pecking order' that pervades a range of distinct diplomatic practices. We argue that his account of the pecking order is less a product of his analytical focus on practices and more a product of looking closely at everyday life and the meaning-making that surrounds it. What makes the work of Pouliot (and Simmons and Rush Smith) interesting is not the focus on practice (or process) but their willingness to delve into the meaning of such practices or processes, and to explain the ways in which practices (and processes) emerge in response to dilemmas.

Our alternative is to start, both analytically and empirically, with the meanings and beliefs of situated agents. It is their views that are key to providing a decentred explanation of the social world. What we need is a way of talking about these meanings and beliefs across contexts, drawing out patterns of similarity and difference as we go. Dilemmas, we suggest, provide an answer to that conundrum. Focusing on dilemmas can give the analyst insight into common factors unveiled in a process-orientated approach, while also allowing the analyst to tease out key patterns of everyday practice.

Our distinction between Big-D and small-d is a useful device for guiding empirical researchers applying interpretive theory. Our privileging of small-d dilemmas, in this sense, represents a desire for interpretive researchers to escape from the constraints of mainstream comparative frameworks. In reality, of course, Big-D and small-d dilemmas are often intimately intertwined. Indeed, the small-d dilemmas which confront actors in practice frequently stem from tensions wrought by clashing traditions. Take, for example, Bernardo Zacka's (2017) account of the moral dilemmas facing street-level bureaucrats in a welfare non-profit organisation in a large American city. He shows in colourful detail how the dilemmas that bureaucrats face – most pointedly, whether to turn away unscheduled clients or squeeze appointments in – reflect conflicting moral dispositions 'designed in' to their organisation through layers of ideologically contested welfare reform. The everyday small-d dilemma experienced by the bureaucrat is the concrete manifestation of the fundamental Big-D dilemmas which shape their organisation and work (Corbett 2017; see also Geddes 2018).

In our own case, then, as analysts, we might eventually link Edna's and Tony's predicaments to Big-D dilemmas: how beliefs about austerity clash with beliefs about inclusive growth; how the institutions of electoral representation clash with the demands of governing in a small and poor country. In fact, the seemingly mundane dilemma of whether to catch the village bus might reveal in acute fashion the perennial and dramatic clash between competing beliefs about who ought to be responsible for lifting people out of poverty and how. We might even tease these links out by reflecting with Edna and Tony themselves, or other participants who have expressed similar stories and sentiments. Our contention is merely that we are more likely to reveal interesting and unexpected insights when we start where the actors do – with the difficult choices they have to make. In many cases the link between Big-D and small-d dilemmas will be imposed by the analyst rather than emerge from participants themselves.

How Does a Focus on Dilemmas Enable Comparison in Practice?

For comparative interpretive research, the crucial point is that actors in different contexts – like Tony and Edna – can articulate remarkably similar dilemmas. The similarities between dilemmas allows interpretive researchers to develop plausible conjectures that may or may resonate beyond the immediate context in which they are initially developed. Schaffer (2015: 7), for example, argues that the goal of interpretive concept formation is to 'investigate the ways in which the social world is built up linguistically and the ways in which social actors deploy concepts to pursue their goals'. Despite interviews being conducted in English, both Tony and Edna use different language to explain their dilemmas. But their similar aspirations – economic development for remote island communities – provide a common ground for comparing their experience. Leaving open the possibility that plausible conjectures may travel, across time and space, is essential to providing decentred explanations as it elides the reification of context. To be sure, plausible conjectures can never function as formal laws in the way naturalists imagine. They are not generalisable or predictive and, while they are abstracted from experience, they cannot be isolated from their unique context (see also Adcock 2006: 62). But they can be more or less analogous, allowing us to draw out parallels and affinities between even the most disparate circumstances.

Drilling down into those dilemmas – what generates them, and how actors respond to them in different contexts – also structures and guides the comparative exploration and analysis. Intensive interpretive research teases out dilemmas, explores the beliefs that underpin them and identifies how they explain political action. Again, we suggest that the juxtaposition of Edna's and Tony's stories reveals how a focus on small-d dilemmas in particular can enable exciting new forms of comparison.

Focusing on Big-D dilemmas does not preclude any form of interpretive comparison. *Comparing Westminster* is a case in point. It uses a form of comparing that is not radically different in look and feel from a mainstream emphasis on comparative institutions. Indeed, an analyst who starts with a traditional comparative approach across Westminster countries might end up at a similar set of insights and conclusions., Donald Savoie's (1999 and 2008) comparative analysis of Canada and the UK echoes much of what Rhodes, Wanna and Weller find in *Comparing Westminster*. That is because the 'traditions' at the centre of Big-D dilemmas can resemble or mirror the institutional, cultural or ideational variables that structure mainstream comparative research. In fact, as we will stress in Chapter 4, it is important to start with anticipated Big-D dilemmas before entering the field, because they can help structure the initial design of a research project in ways that mainstream reviewers and funding bodies will recognise and find attractive.

Nevertheless, it is a focus on small-d dilemmas that opens up a more radical and creative form of comparison. Tony and Edna are so different that mainstream approaches to social science would never think to compare everyday low-income residents on the South Coast of England and elite political actors in the Pacific Islands. Nonetheless, their shared dilemmas reveal surprising similarities in their experiences – both are victims of a precarious island isolation and the stresses and strains that come with it – but also differences in their normative preferences and in the consequences flowing from their responses. The comparison places the exoticism of far-flung Pacific Islands in the context of mundane transportation logistics, while at the same time revealing the apparently archetypal English social housing estate as an unexpectedly exotic site of geographical and social isolation. We see both contexts in a new and potentially penetrating light.

Understanding how dilemmas – especially the small-d dilemmas of every-day practice – *can* enable comparison is not the same as understanding how to go about doing such comparison. Indeed, our juxtaposition of vignettes reveals that there are a multitude of ways to make comparisons. The comparison between Edna and Tony could be about the politics of globalisation and isolation; islands and islanders; transport and infrastructure develop-ment; social welfare; or democratic representation. It could be a study grounded in a distinct discipline (e.g. political science; political geography; political economy; planning and urban studies) or in area studies (British studies; Pacific studies; or island studies). A focus on dilemmas opens up creative possibilities but provides no set recipe to structure that comparative analysis. We hope Chapters 4–7 can offer pragmatic advice to shape and guide that creative journey. We devote the rest of this chapter, though, to the practical task of identifying and exploring the dilemmas at the heart of the enterprise.

How Do We Identify and Explore Dilemmas in Practice?

For Chapter 3–7, a key notion in our analysis is 'rules of thumb'. We follow conventional usage – they are a guide based on practice. They are a broadly accurate compass that allows us to see the wood through the trees. They guide our journey on the map provided by our plausible conjectures. We call them rules of thumb because they draw attention to the types of choices researchers have to make; they do not provide the last word (see also Gerring

Table 3.2 Rules of thumb for comparing dilemmas

1. Develop an initial 'roadmap' of potential dilemmas
2. But be prepared to toss the map aside
3. Uncover local formulations of dilemmas
4. But 'own' your interpretation
5. Embrace empathy and intuition
6. But ally empathy with humility
7. Scout creative possibilities for comparison across contexts
8. But establish the limits of your comparison

2017). They are not true or false, right or wrong, but more or less helpful in seeking out plausible conjectures in the field, and in fostering new ideas. Echoing the purpose of the book, they help to demystify the process of doing comparative interpretive research. At the same time, the term 'rules of thumb' helps us retain a sense that each project is different and each researcher will creatively adjust the rules to the context in which they are working. They will adjust them also to resolve the logistical and emotional challenges of doing their own comparative fieldwork project. We list the rules of thumb for the study of dilemmas in Table 3.2.

Rule 1: Develop an Initial 'Roadmap' of Potential Dilemmas

We do not go into the field seeking confirmation of a pre-existing list of dilemmas. However, we do need at least a preliminary road map, some plausible conjectures, of what we might be looking for (Schwartz-Shea and Yanow 2012). We will revise, even discard, that list later (see Rule #2). But the initial 'roadmap' sharpens our inquiry and guides our fieldwork.

There are many ways of unearthing potential dilemmas in the initial 'deskwork' phase of a research project. One is documentary analysis. When Corbett began interviewing politicians like Tony, he was not surprised that they experienced a dilemma in how and how often to access their constituency because he had read around fifty autobiographical/biographical accounts by Pacific leaders. Many of these texts made the same point, albeit with nuances that reflected the era they were from, their age, gender, electoral strategy and support base and so on. Interviews and 'being there' – in a bar, late at night, far from home – brought the magnitude and depth of feeling associated with the dilemma into sharp relief, but the initial deskwork meant that Corbett was already attuned to its significance.

Another way of anticipating dilemmas, especially important where the documentary record is threadbare, is to draw on personal experience. Preparations for the fieldwork for Boswell's study of deprivation on England's south coast (Edna's dilemma) is a good example. Boswell's own experience was not much use. His previous research had primarily involved elite actors. And, though he had spent a short period of his childhood in the region, he had predominantly lived elsewhere, and always in relative middle-class comfort. (Tales like Edna's, as we will elaborate later, were to be confronting, confounding, affecting experiences). But the project brought together a research team with a variety of life and research experiences which helped prepare them for the task. One of the researchers was completing a PhD thesis in a similar topic, and so had recent fieldwork from which to draw parallels. Another had grown up in the region in a context of deprivation and could reflect on his own background. Moreover, the research funder, the Joseph Rowntree Foundation (JRF) – a charity devoted to the alleviation of poverty in the UK – had a hands-on role in steering the project. JRF representatives could call on a wealth of experience investigating the effects of inequality, the consequences of austerity and so on, across the UK (albeit little of this work touched on the historically affluent south coast region). Initial team meetings involved sharing these experiences to develop a list of anticipated dilemmas – we expected our participants to articulate hard choices between being unemployed or taking up precarious work in the 'gig economy', or to reflect on the dilemma of moving for opportunity or staying close to family roots. These dilemmas informed the case selection, planned interview topic guide and initial field observations. They offered a roadmap to begin the journey. But experience in the field would tilt the angle of inquiry – the key point we turn to next.

Rule 2: But Be Prepared to Toss the Map Aside

Interpretive research is, fundamentally, guided by the 'logic of discovery' and open to the prospect of surprise. We should expect that the initial 'roadmap' will only get us so far, especially in a complex comparative project. An emphasis on dilemmas is an excellent way of channelling this process of exploration. The chief benefit of a focus on dilemmas is that it hones in on the way people see their choices in their everyday life and on the ways in which they construct meanings to makes sense of them. We focus on what emerges from engagement in the field. Certainly, in our experience, it is the dilemmas that actors voice that typically capture our attention and interest.

Their dilemmas are what leave both them and us puzzling in the mutual effort to make meaning.

So, when Corbett spoke with politicians like Tony in the Pacific, they spent little time on mundane questions about the technical aspects of legislation or the procedures for responding to constituent enquiries. Instead, invariably, they shifted the conversation to focus on the dilemmas presented by the conflicting expectations of actors around them, or the competing demands on their time and resources. One of the key questions they discussed was why, given the exorbitant personal and financial costs of being a politician, they kept running for elections. As the opening vignette illustrates, many of the politicians talked about how conflicted they were on this question. By puzzling together about their options and choices, they sought to give meaning for their continued participation in a set of political practices and processes that many of them were deeply ambivalent about. Capturing these meanings, and the ambivalence, became a central theme in the subsequent book (Corbett 2015a).

Likewise, when Boswell reported in a steering committee meeting for the south coast project that transportation logistics were emerging as *the* key issue in the research, he was initially met with incredulity. The response was that surely there were more significant issues impacting on people's lives – housing, employment, access to health and welfare services? However, an emphasis on dilemmas revealed that mundane transport logistics were at the heart of all these broader issues that the research team had anticipated. For Edna – and many like her - getting a job, moving house, seeing the doctor all hinged on whether it was worth catching the hopeless bus service. In other words, the initial research 'roadmap', though not entirely inaccurate, was missing crucial detail that only an open-ended focus on dilemmas could uncover.

Rule 3: Uncover Local Formulations of Dilemmas

We know when we come across a dilemma in the field because our research participants, like Edna and Tony, identify it and reflect on it. The analytical sense in which we use the term dilemma, drawn from interpretive theory, is entirely consistent with the everyday sense of the term – that is, a dilemma entails making a choice between two or more alternative (and often undesirable) courses of action.

As this might suggest, a principal advantage of the term dilemma is that it is commonly used in everyday (English) language. Obviously, not all actors will use it, and the term may not translate perfectly across contexts. Edna, for instance, never used the word dilemma in our interactions. But she used a variety of phrases which expressed a similar sentiment. She talked about being 'damned if you do, and damned if you don't'. She felt at times life was like 'banging your head against a brick wall'. She shrugged her shoulders and asked, 'What can you do?' Corbett's politicians like Tony talked about their 'challenges' and 'problems', or the 'conflict' they experienced between, for example, the demands of their constituency and their legally mandated role as elected representatives. As this might suggest, there are many synonyms or near synonyms for 'dilemma'. There are quandaries, Catch 22s, contradictions, predicaments, impasses, problems, puzzles and tight spots. Insiders may well have their own language. They may experience 'little local difficulties' or protest 'crisis what crisis' or refer to 'events'. Such phrases signal the possibility of an unresolved dilemma. There will always be several 'language games' (Wittgenstein 2009 [1953]) each of which is context dependent. To uncover the various meanings, we rely on interview questions about the main topics of conversation and disagreement. Equally, we can draw on public records of debates, documentary research, and media interviews and archives. We explore such sources to prompt interviewees about dilemmas.

Rule 4: But 'Own' Your Interpretation

One of the appeals of an analytical focus on dilemmas is that it is close to lay terminology. We can be confident in comparing dilemmas across contexts precisely because actors, like Edna and Tony, articulate them in similar ways. They are not hidden or impenetrable constructs of the analyst. They are not plucked out of thin air. They need to make sense to our participants, and mimic or echo the way they make sense of them. But inevitably, and unashamedly, this work involves abstracting from individual experience and imposing our own interpretation, especially when we seek to compare. Interpretive research cannot reveal 'true' experience. Our findings are inevitably our interpretations of other people's interpretations. In this sense, the respective dilemmas of catching a bus (every day) and taking a boat (occasionally) in our vignettes cannot be said to be exactly the same. But we judge that they are similar enough that we can use the abstract idea to make interesting and robust comparisons. We are clear and transparent about what we are doing and why. Readers can make their own judgements.

Nevertheless, it is important to acknowledge that the dilemmas interpretive researchers encounter in practice might be rather messier or less clear-cut than those in our exemplars. The bus and the boat are concrete objects. Getting on or staying off are unambiguous binaries. But the dilemmas of everyday experience also occur in relation to abstract notions and can present multifaceted or multi-dimensional choices. Take, for example, the vignettes Maynard-Moody and Musheno (2000) provide from their field-work at the beginning of an influential paper on street-level bureaucrats. The first is of a senior police officer struggling in an encounter to overcome the fear and suspicion of an African American woman requiring assistance; the second of a care worker recalling her efforts to help an elderly woman access available treatments for her failing eyesight. Neither situation is precisely the same. Scholars in policing and social care might be tempted to situate them in their idiographic context, and tease out and emphasise their specific entanglements. But the authors prefer to abstract from these experiences the 'fundamental dilemma, perhaps the defining characteristic, of street-level work . . . that the needs of individual citizen-clients exist in tension with the demands and limits of rules' (Maynard-Moody and Musheno 2000: 349). It is this dilemma in practice that occupies their discussion and analysis. Was the abstraction from these two particular experiences to a more widespread dilemma legitimate? Was the sacrifice in idiographic richness worth it? We certainly think so, and the countless others who include this by now 'classic' on postgraduate reading lists would seem to agree.

Rule #5: Embrace Empathy and Intuition

Naturalist research seeks to control empathy and other human emotions. When seeking to uncover dilemmas, empathy and other emotions are essential tools. We do not have to like our research participants – although often we do. We do not have to be friends with them. We do have to stand in their shoes to see some of their world (Reeher 2006) and to appreciate their vantage point. It is impossible to identify dilemmas otherwise. Empathy is thus essential to this type of research (cf. Corbett 2014).

Though it is possible to empathise from a distance, it comes much more naturally in the field. The experience of the context and the interaction with participants can be arresting, disruptive, affecting. Indeed, in our examples, Edna and Tony's dilemma was something we experienced acutely (albeit only fleetingly) ourselves. Boswell became a slave to the No. 6 bus during field-work on the Isle of Wight. He spent hours waiting in dreary bus shelters. He fretted about fitting interviews in with the timetable. He cursed having to cough up a mammoth taxi fare when his connection was delayed. He had to weigh up the cost of missing the bus versus the cost of missing out on valuable data when a focus group discussion threatened to overrun. Corbett maintains he only appreciated the vastness of the Pacific Ocean – nearly half of the world's water surface – after criss-crossing it, albeit in an airplane. Likewise, he appreciated how disconnected from regular transport links many of these island nations are when he was sick, and desperate to get home, but the next flight was days away. We do not raise these experiences to arouse sympathy. They were little more than a mild inconvenience. But their urgency and immediacy in that context helped to put in perspective the everyday dilemma Edna, Tony and our other participants were voicing. We *felt* (only a little of) their anxiety.

Rule #6: But Ally Empathy with Humility

We have argued that the small-d dilemmas of everyday practice are crucial to unlocking surprising or interesting comparison. The trouble is that it can be hard to gain and maintain the sort of access necessary to identify and understand the everyday dilemmas of research participants. Appearing empathetic and seeking to build trust is crucial in terms of a general approach to fieldwork. Yet, we are often suspicious of interpretive researchers for being overly empathetic towards their participants and that this intimacy undermines objectivity. This age-old concern has been revisited recently in the often-visceral reaction to Goffman's award-winning ethnography *On the Run: Fugitive Life in an American City* (2014), an ethnographic account of how mass incarcerations and policing practices shaped low-income African-American urban communities' understandings of the police and the criminal justice system. Lubet (2018: xii), claims 'that Goffman's account of social reality has been influenced by her identification with her subjects, while her progressive agenda ... had compromised her objectivity' (see also Worley, Worley and Wood 2016).

This concern only makes sense if Goffman's work is placed within a naturalist paradigm where the analyst can and should view their research and research subjects with clinical dispassion. As will be clear by now, we do not see these standards as plausible or desirable. As we will discuss at length in the next chapter, the reflexive normative preferences of the researcher are the key to interpreting any study and so they should be embraced, not be suppressed or controlled for. But, having said that, we do not think that having or developing empathy for our participants is problem free. Rather, we see the primary danger as a tendency to become overwhelmed with empathy, and to assume a capacity to speak *for* rather than *through* participants. The impulse is well-intentioned, but risks patronising them and the nuances of their stories and experiences.

This risk is especially great in a comparative account where one person's account is juxtaposed with somebody else from another time or place that they do not know and probably do not care too much about. Tony and Edna have never met. Perhaps if they did, they would recognise their shared dilemmas but they might also see each other's circumstances as entirely foreign and exotic. Ultimately, we have used their stories and experiences to tell our story, for our purposes. While we have sought to portray them as empathetically as we could, we cannot and do not speak for them – they are perfectly capable of doing that for themselves! And yet, even quoting them at length in our texts does not completely absolve us of this problem either. Ultimately, it is our account, we speak *through* them, and this awareness should engender a degree of humility as we work.

Rule 7: Scout Creative Possibilities for Comparison Across Contexts

The rules of thumb we have articulated thus far implicitly help to identify and explore dilemmas in a comparative project, rather than a single case. To make comparison explicit Anderson (2016: 130) argues we should ask ourselves the simple question: are there fundamental similarities and differences in the dilemmas actors experience across contexts? Do actors in one location experience the same dilemma as those in another? Do they experience the dilemma at the same time? Do dilemmas travel across social fields: gender, age, race or class? The kaleidoscope metaphor is important when conducting this type of research. As we change the focus, what about our understanding of the phenomena under study remains, and what falls away? We can look for differences in the dilemmas actors experience, or differences in the way they respond across contexts we might expect to be similar. More profitably still, in the vein of our comparison of Edna and Tony, we can do so by looking at similarities across contexts we might expect to be different.

In this sense, the initial inspiration for comparing the village bus and the island boat was not the product of some monk-like indwelling (as in idiographic folklore) nor of any systematically designed comparison (as in naturalist textbooks). It emerged during one of Boswell and Corbett's regular, rambling chats over a cup of tea. Boswell was reflecting on some of the unexpected or surprising issues emerging from his continuing study of the lived experience of poverty on England's affluent south coast when Corbett noted strong affinities with his body of work in the remote Pacific Islands.

As such, the creative process that inspired and drove the comparison was a product of an inevitable feature of comparative interpretive research – *yo-yo fieldwork* (we expand on this point in Chapter 5). That is to say, there is a pragmatic need to 'yo-yo' between fieldwork and deskwork, and in and out of different field settings, to balance different work responsibilities, and other priorities beyond work. The potential affinities across the village bus and island boat contexts emerged as Boswell yo-yoed in and out of the field, and in a context where Corbett continues (albeit at a slower rate) to yo-yo back in and out of small island states in the Pacific (and elsewhere). Both had the academic grunt work of teaching and administration to attend to alongside fieldwork. But this patchy and piecemeal reality need not be seen as a poor second-best to the extended ethnographic soak as the anthropological rite of passage. It was what enabled them to juxtapose loosely related ideas and experiences, to have productive conversations, and ultimately to see things in new and interesting ways.

Rule 8: But Establish the Limits of Your Comparison

Both Boswell and Corbett's independent projects entailed multiple sites in their own right. The village bus and island boat dilemmas did not seem to recur uniformly across these sites. This variety speaks to the need to establish the frontiers of comparison. In this case – because the shared dilemma arose by and large *after* the completion of intensive fieldwork phases in both studies – we returned to our respective datasets and established the limits of the common dilemma. We established that the village bus dilemma applied to rural or market town settings but not to urban areas in Boswell's study. Likewise, the island boat was much more of a dilemma in archipelagic Pacific Island states than it was in others canvassed in Corbett's study. The point is that dilemmas are always 'situated' but that the context is not deterministic: it frames the choice but it does not predict what an actor will do. Or, to put it another way, the problem is shared but because actors respond differently, the solution varies.

If we extend the project with more field research, the selection and adaptation of sites will require a further process of puzzling, working out where similar dilemmas emerge and what further forms of comparison might enable us to find and say interesting and important things. That further field research might take place in the South Coast of England or the Pacific Islands to confirm or extend emergent findings, but it could equally take in some-where completely new and different – among, say, pilgrims along the Camino to Santiago de Compostela, or hitch hikers on New Zealand's South Island.

Conclusion

The point of this chapter has been to stress the central role of dilemmas in our account of comparative interpretive research. Of course, no one, not even omniscient authors, can resolve all, or indeed many, dilemmas. No belief system can answer all questions. As researchers, we can only hope to identify and understand the dilemmas, and the way they inform actions. In this chapter, we have shown how to identify dilemmas. The rules of thumb we develop for identifying dilemmas are only the first step in this long, iterative process.

As such, the chapter also serves as a pivot as we move from setting out the conceptual underpinning of our approach to a practical, grounded account of how to conduct research in this fashion. In subsequent chapters, we turn to the question of how to collect the data about dilemmas, how to analyse that data and how to write it up. First, however, we must consider how to design the research and select the cases.

4 Design

The main task of the research plan will be to carry out qualitative fieldwork under a "comparative interpretivist" framework ... It is hard to argue against the proposition that we ought to have more qualitative case studies. But I have serious reservations about how much we can learn from this design, because it suffers from selection bias ... [I therefore] simply do not believe that it can generate the insights that it is meant to generate ... To rescue the project would require a fundamental reconceptualization.

(Anonymous Grant Reviewer)

Choosing two communities in two countries will be like drawing playing cards from two packs. No matter how much is discovered about these four cards, no resemblance to the rest of the deck can be claimed using the proposed method ... In my view, the important questions that this proposal seeks to address could all be better investigated from the vantage-point of a single site.

(Anonymous Grant Reviewer)

Although the talk is explicitly [sic] in terms of a research strategy and research design, this is not political science...

(Review of Rhodes, Wanna and Weller, *Comparing Westminster*, O'Malley 2011: 97)

Three comparative interpretive projects. Three different reviewer responses to our proposed case selection strategy. We are obviously not alone in having our approach to case selection criticised by reviewers. What these quotes do reveal, however, is that although the questions that typically animate discussions of research design are deceptively simple – what should we study and how should we design our research to study it? – answers depend on the research tradition. Naturalist qualitative researchers (see Reviewers 1 and 3 above) adhere to the same goals and principles as quantitative researchers – the mantra is one of 'diverse tools, shared standards' (Brady and Collier 2010). But if the goal of research is generalisable, falsifiable and predictive findings, then getting the initial research design right is imperative for hypothesis testing. Case selection must be designed into the project at its inception, and any change to the design would be tantamount to redesigning the entire project. The default setting is a comparative design which will allow the researcher to isolate, measure and test a theoretical proposition – i.e. the independent variable. In exceptional circumstances, researchers might select cases on the dependent variable and attempt to look within single cases for specific causal mechanisms (see, for example, the contributions to Bennett and Checkel 2015). But, for many, this type of study is said to suffer from an endogeneity problem and therefore findings must be subjected to specific tests to ensure they are generalisable and predictive. So, most mainstream accounts of small–medium N case selection continue to be dominated by some variant or extension of John Stuart Mills' 'method of difference' (for discussion see Lijphart 1971).

For humanists or interpretivists (see Reviewer 2 above), on the other hand, case study research represents a distinct alternative to the naturalist paradigm underpinning quantitative social science (e.g. Flyvbjerg 2006). Drawing inspiration from the humanities – history and anthropology especially – these scholars aim at 'thick description' rather than rigid generalisability (see Geertz 1973). The mantra is that 'small facts speak to large issues' – that the insights from in-depth case research can generate plausible conjectures of broad theoretical applicability or at least interest. What this means is that interpretivists also have a much more ambivalent view of case selection and research design. In fact, thinkers as influential as Schwartz-Shea and Yanow (2012) tend to eschew the language of case selection altogether. They see notions of 'case selection' as investing a false sense of control in the researcher who, in practice, remains inextricably bound by his or her own subjective biases, limited knowledge and pragmatic limitations:

The selection of cases according to a 'most similar' or 'most different' design logics assumes that what is 'similar' and 'different' can be determined by an external judge, the researcher. (Schwartz-Shea and Yanow 2012: 147, n16)

The implied default in interpretive research design, then, is idiographic. As Soss (2018) puts it pithily, interpretivists don't study a case, they case a study. The task of the researcher is to work out exactly what theirs is a case of through a process of abductive reasoning. What Soss means is that an interpretive orientation, in the logic of exploration, is focused mostly on working out what exactly an in-depth study is a case of (rather than assuming and asserting this *a priori*). We agree, and it pervades the way we have written about our own single case work (see, for example, Boswell 2018).

This division is overly stylised. If political scientists were exclusively theory driven then the discipline would not be so empirically wedded to the study of a few large, rich, western states (Veenendaal and Corbett 2015). Likewise, area studies scholars still have to choose what they study *within* their case – which region or social group, election or coup, for example – and so the menu of what their research is a case *of* tends to be narrower than it might first appear. What the distinction does reveal, however, is that discussion of *what* we should study and *how* we should conduct research is inseparable from two other key questions underpinning any such pursuit: namely *why* we are undertaking a research project, and *where* we should begin a research project.

Addressing the why question gets at the fundamental normative preferences underpinning the research. In the naturalist tradition, the underlying motivation is to make a theoretical contribution – to expose or challenge a prevailing orthodoxy, to lend weight to one side of a debate or to generate an entirely new explanation. There are always normative commitments but they are buried behind the overriding normative commitment to 'science'. Choices about case selection, within the existing, sophisticated menu, stem from this predilection.

In the interpretive tradition, there is often greater reflexivity about the normative aspirations of the research. The interpretive commitment to acknowledging positionality sees all decisions about *what* we choose to study and *how* we go about doing research as unavoidably normative in nature. Therefore, the key task is to spell out the experiences and beliefs that motivated the research and inflect the fieldwork, analysis and interpretation. What we choose to compare is inextricably linked to *why* we are interested in comparing in the first place (see Anderson 2016). So, Corbett (2015a) compares between different Pacific states because he wants to push back against prevailing scholarly ideas that political action in these countries is determined by timeless cultural traditions that are essentially pre-modern in nature. But he also compares because he wants to make a bold and encompassing counterargument against the dominant agenda around good governance in the region, questioning the widespread assumption that political corruption, self-interest and incompetence are holding back economic development. Comparative interpretive research, in this sense, requires acknowledging positionality both personally (our moral and political commitments) and professionally (our desire to make an impression on the field). Embracing these different sources of motivation has fundamental implications for how we might understand case selection.

Case Selection Strategies for Comparative Interpretive Research

While we are obviously sympathetic to the view that interpretive research should not have to conform to the same standards as naturalist social science, we also acknowledge the general ambivalence of many researchers in this tradition towards explicitly comparative projects. We are not alone. There are increasing calls for interpretive researchers to look beyond the emphasis on single cases, at least on occasion (Anderson 2016; Robinson 2011; Simmons and Smith 2015). Yet researchers like us who do this work are left to fumble around when trying to explain and justify our cases for comparison. We can be left with an unpalatable choice between shoe-horning in ill-fitting 'case selection strategies' grounded in positivist assumptions, or obscuring the comparative element of the project altogether. As the quotes we started with illustrate, the outcome is often equally displeasing to both sides of the methodological divide. It is too 'soft' for the naturalists seeking to control for confounding variables across context. It is too 'hard' for the interpretivists concerned about flattening context or omitting the prospect of surprise by structuring the comparisons.

What is needed, and what we seek to provide in this chapter, is a distinctively *interpretive* language for adopting and adapting comparative case selection. As this suggests, we need an approach to comparative case selection that recognises the inherently *abductive* nature of interpretive research. In other words, a distinctly interpretive language for comparative case selection needs to reflect the interpretivist commitment to moving back and forth between theory and empirics as a project evolves. Interpretivists work out iteratively the precise nature of the empirical focus and what that focus means in theoretical terms. Interpretive researchers cannot control for confounding variables in the initial design of a project (as in the influential accounts of Gerring 2006 or Yin 2014); nor would we want to. A commitment to abduction means recognising that a researcher cannot know what those variables are in advance. The whole point of immersive fieldwork in detailed case research is that it is potentially transformative, admitting and celebrating the prospect of surprise and discovery. How we understand and justify comparison, in these terms, needs to evolve as the research project evolves.

This recognition of the centrality of abduction requires, in practice, a commitment to iteration, to 'sucking and seeing' while researchers confront and navigate the messy complexities that any project unveils. We cannot possibly provide a simple 'recipe book' or 'formula' for justifying comparison akin to popular positivist accounts. What we can offer is three broad 'strategies' and associated rules of thumb that might guide interpretivists as they seek to carry out this type of research. The important point, however, and the one upon which our contribution turns, is that because interpretive research is abductive, we will need different strategies for different phases of a comparative project. Like all scholars, we have to start somewhere and we find many of the strategies proposed by more naturalist orientated scholars useful for the initial task of approaching a topic. Because our research projects are open-ended and iterative, we also need strategies for changing or adding cases mid-way through, and for re-purposing what our research is a case *of* once we have collected data. Despite the overwhelming body of literature on this topic, this emphasis on different case selection strategies – particularly different comparative case selection strategies - for different phases of research is unique. The key takeaway is that for comparative interpretive research, altering, amending or augmenting your case selection is not the sign of a failed initial design; it is the essence of good abductive research.

Our three case selection strategies are:

- *Provisional*: comparative projects need to start somewhere We see no harm in borrowing some of the language common to the naturalist tradition at the beginning of a project. But, we also suggest being explicit about your normative preferences as a researcher. Specifically, as outlined in Chapter 3, you should provisionally decide whether you are *mostly* interested in uncovering similarities or differences across disparate contexts.
- *Adaptive*: to undertake abductive research we need to remain open to surprise and the potential for empirical findings to fundamentally alter our topic, questions and design. Therefore, once we enter the field we suggest a strategy built around the possibility of analogous discoveries. The key here is to follow where you are led.
- *Reflective*: because abductive projects never end, we will also often need to reconsider and potentially re-justify our case selection once we have collected our data, seek to publish our findings for different audiences or collaborate with other scholars by combining fieldwork material.

An analytical emphasis on the dilemmas that actors face is the key to pursuing this flexible approach. Before a project starts, we can intuit and imagine the important dilemmas at the centre of the research puzzle. This is

Table 4.1 Rules of thumb for research design and case study selection

Comparative strategy	Rules of thumb for case selection
Provisional *Key question*: Are you mostly interested in discovering similarities or differences?	*Before data collection* 1. Choose intrinsically interesting cases. 2. Make your normative preferences explicit 3. Pragmatically consider logistics and audience(s)
Adaptive *Key question*: Are your emerging findings consistent with your provisional design, or does your design need to be altered to incorporate insights from the field?	*During data collection* 4. Embrace the creative intuition 5. Follow where you are led and take what you can get
Reflective *Key question*: Are there eclectic affinities (or discrepancies) that could be drawn out for different audiences or with new collaborators?	*After data collection* 6. Remember the project never 'ends' 7. Collaborate to increase the number of cases

a best-laid plan, founded in what we are initially trying to achieve (our initial response to the 'why' question). But delving into the field, and encountering the unexpected and counter-intuitive dilemmas that inevitably crop up in practice, can alter our understandings, beliefs and normative preferences. It sparks alternative possibilities. This messy and often confusing process encourages us to adapt or augment the initial plan. It pushes us towards adding or switching comparative cases, shifting emphasis within an existing design or even dropping preconceived comparisons altogether. The following rules of thumb offer a guide through this iterative and messy process (see Table 4.1).

Before Data Collection

Rule #1: Choose Intrinsically Interesting Cases

As outlined, in recent decades the case study, including the single case study, has undergone something of a revival in certain sections of political science. Whereas the development of increasingly sophisticated quantitative techniques threatened to obliterate political science case studies because they could not produce robust – generalisable and predictive – findings, the counter-revolution has emphasised the value of in-depth descriptive work for naturalist political science (see Flyvbjerg 2006; Gerring 2004, 2006; Yin 2014). Whether by 'process tracing' (George and Bennett 2005) or undertaking qualitative comparative analysis (Ragin 2009), naturalist political science has carved out a growing niche for qualitative and mixed methods research designs.

The value of this revival is that it has refined the menu of ways in which cases might be justified when designing a project in any research tradition. For example, Seawright and Gerring (2008: 297–298) provide five 'methods' of case selection – typical; diverse, extreme, deviant; and influential – in addition to the more common 'most similar' and 'most different' (Lijphart 1971) strategies. There are, of course, variations on these lists. Flyvbjerg (2006), for example, includes 'paradigmatic' cases, which have affinities with 'influential' cases. In other disciplines, like human geography (see McFarlane and Robinson 2012), a revived interest in comparative case selection covers similar ground but with different labels: 'universalising', 'encompassing', 'variation-finding', etc. Each language has its merits.

We see no need to reinvent this discussion or create our own language. Rather, in keeping with our belief that this initial thinking is provisional only, we offer two main points of departure for interpretivists setting out on a comparative project: First, as will be clear by now, we reject the claim that the goal of research design, and by extension case selection, is generalisability and predictability. As a result, while we are essentially agnostic about using naturalist language for case justification, we do not share the belief that we must select cases because they are 'typical' or 'deviant', etc. Rather, we see the empirical task as determining *how* a case is in fact 'typical' or 'deviant'. The emphasis on *how* is important because we would not expect any comparison between cases – defined here in any number of ways, from a single event, individual, institution, country, era etc. – to be completely similar or completely different. Our philosophical assumptions mean that we expect cases to have weaker or stronger affinities along multiple dimensions. We expect all comparison between cases to be kaleidoscopic, presenting several pictures of a contested 'reality'. The empirical task is to explore, compare and contrast the overlapping pictures as we change the standpoint from which we inspect the narratives.

Having said that, no researcher approaches a case with a blank mind. As scholars, we are all interested in cases precisely because we think they might well be 'typical', 'deviant', etc. of the phenomenon we want to study. The lists compiled by authors such as Lijphart, Flyvbjerg, Gerring and Seawright, and Robinson act as a neat device for discerning what it is about the case we want to study that makes it interesting. We often find it beneficial to engage in this type of thinking before we begin our research. However, we would not want to be restricted by these categories. We will expand on this point when we discuss how a case can be 'typical' and 'deviant' at the same time, depending on the literature to which we seek to contribute. For now, we simply caution against a rigid approach to research design and case selection that stifles creative, discovery-orientated intuition from the outset. Changing what the data are a case of in order to make the research interesting is relatively straightforward but if learning about the case is tedious, then the study is unlikely to produce empirically rich research.

Rule #2: Make Your Normative Preferences Explicit

Our second point of departure from the naturalist approach to research design and case selection is the emphasis we place on foregrounding your normative preferences. Like naturalists, we are interested in similarities and differences between cases. But, as above, we do not presume or 'design' these similarities or differences into the project from the beginning as this would close off the creative and discovery-orientated value of our research. We have hunches about whether cases are in fact 'typical', or 'deviant', and about the types of dilemmas that they will reveal. But, these hunches are not necessarily born out of a desire to test particular theories. More often, we posit, they are born out of particular personal normative preferences that we have for our research and the argument we want to prosecute in our writing.

A naturalist orientation, with its emphasis on mimicking the natural sciences implicitly or explicitly, seeks to suppress or control for the researchers' normative preferences by privileging theoretically motivated justifications. It is not that scholars who work in this tradition do not have personal normative preferences but rather the concern is that such preferences might bias the findings. Our approach takes the opposite view. We assume that all research is biased by the researcher's normative preferences (see also MacIntyre 1972). The only question is how reflexive the researcher is about that bias, and how honest and forthcoming they are with their audience(s) about why they are doing research on their chosen topic. Moreover, rather than compromise the validity of our findings, we believe that the personal normative preferences we bring to the study enliven and enrich the research we do.

Weapons of the Weak is an exemplar. This book would not work if James C. Scott (1985) were not cheering for the peasants. Or, if we were to pick on our own work, Corbett's (2015a) *Being Political* would not make sense if we did not know from the start that he thought the way scholars and aid donors caricature politicians was unfair and unhelpful. Our personal normative preferences drive our projects, whether we admit it or not. We are not detached observers, impartially weighing conflicting accounts. We might be more or less wedded to particular normative aspects of our projects. We might change our minds about the normative value of what we are doing once we get going. At the heart of interpretive research is a belief that *our rendering* of the story matters. It is the enthusiasm that readers find compelling about a work like *Weapons of the Weak*, even if they do not agree with the assumptions or the findings. The reason the topic is of interest and the research is conducted matters. The pretence of controlling for bias is unedifying.

Rule #3: Pragmatically Consider Logistics and Audience(s)

Our final rule to note before commencing data collection is that, while we have emphasised that researchers should follow their creative intuition when designing their projects, rather than seeking to force their interests into a rigid design, this enthusiasm must be tempered with a healthy dose of pragmatism. Indeed, as we will discuss further in Chapter 5, pragmatism is perhaps more significant for explicitly comparative interpretive projects as they generally entail additional logistical complexity. In which case, pragmatism should be central to our research design and case selection strategy. If the availability of time or funds for in-depth fieldwork is an issue, then an ethnographic study of the most interesting and normatively salient case in the world probably is not going to be the right one. Likewise, a lack of appropriate language skills may mean it is better to move on to another case. Of course, not all choices are this straightforward. A researcher might have the time and language skills but not the funds, for example. In which case, there are potentially ways to overcome that barrier and proceed with the project.

Whether the project can be done is the most obvious pragmatic restraint, but a less discussed, yet still important, consideration is whether anyone will care whether it gets done even if it can be completed. Much of the rest of this chapter is about how you alter a research design throughout a project to draw out the most interesting and compelling findings. So, while we do not want to belabour this point, or discourage researchers from attempting projects only they value, we are conscious that we live in a world in which PhDs need to get jobs, early career researchers need to get tenure, tenured scholars want to get promoted and famous professors want to consolidate their reputations. In all of these cases, having an audience is incredibly important. Of course, each of us can speak to multiple audiences, which change over time, but it is not a bad idea to think about audiences from the outset (see also Chapter 7).

On a pragmatic level, this matters because if, for example, a researcher aims to contribute to debates in Sinology, but does not have the time or disposition to gain the requisite language skills, then this might not be the best audience for their work. On the other hand, there are numerous examples of mainstream political scientists and international relations scholars who do not speak Mandarin, and yet still write about China, or use it as one of their cases, to make a contribution to disciplinary debates. We can contest the merits of their scholarship, but there is no doubting they still find an audience for their work. Our simple point is that having an idea about who the intended audience is, and the norms and conventions that determine what is published in the reputable journals in that field, is an important consideration when choosing what to study and how to study it. *The China Journal* is much less likely to accept work that does not utilise Mandarin sources than *Comparative Political Studies*, for example. In career terms, this is an important consideration, both for how to describe the project and its contribution, but also the type of department in which a researcher is likely to get a job and attain tenure. The desire might be to do both: publish in area studies and disciplinary journals (as we advocate in Chapter 7). By and large, the more explicitly comparative the work, the harder it becomes to meet the criteria of both audiences because there is an unavoidable trade-off between depth and breadth. So, while these considerations should not become a straightjacket that stifles the comparative intuition, working backwards from the end game is sensible from the outset.

In sum, the naturalist ideal for research design and case selection is that key choices are made before data collection commences and are made based on theoretically salient hypotheses derived from the literature. We demur and instead posit that we should design our research so that it is interesting and fits with our personal normative preferences. That is not to say that thinking through case selection strategies – 'typical', 'deviant' and so on – is unhelpful or even antithetical to good interpretive research. Thinking about what the research is a case of is clearly important to all research traditions. But, we must also acknowledge that these characterisations are provisional only. The same data can be many different types of case depending on the contribution each of us wants to make. In which case, we posit that researchers are more likely to harness their creative intuition if they adopt an adaptive approach. Rather than formal classifications and methods of inference, the main handbrake on creativity should be a healthy dose of pragmatism about what type of material can meaningfully be collected and how the audience will receive it. Other than that, most of the important choices about research design and case selection will be made once the research gets going.

During Data Collection

Rule #4: Embrace the Creative Intuition

Naturalist folklore on research design typically ends here. The hypothesis is formed, the test cases chosen, and now the only task is to collect the material, analyse the results and arrive at findings. Of course, few scholars, of any research tradition, find that their research unfolds this way. Alternatively, if their first project did, it is unlikely that every piece of research they conduct, or every dissertation they supervise for that matter, will adhere to this ideal. We suspect that adapting, revising, redesigning and retrospectively refitting are core business for most social scientists. But, few of us explain the research process this way because by and large this messy and somewhat chaotic picture implies there was a failure in the initial design.

Interpretivist scholars have long held the opposite view that adapting, revising, redesigning and retrospectively refitting are the sign of a project taking shape rather than a failure of planning and execution. As we will discuss in the next chapter, the whole point of going to the field is to be confronted with new and surprising things. Here, we are concerned with how that confrontation affects the justification for the research design and case selection. Bent Flyvbjerg (2006) sums up this experience, and the approach to case selection it implies, when reflecting on his study of local power relations in Aalborg, Denmark (Flyvbjerg 1998). Initially, he conceived of Aalborg as a 'most likely' (Lijphart 1971), 'critical' (Eckstein 1975) or what Gerring (2007) would later call a 'pathway' case, on the grounds that it was widely considered a stronghold of the rational planning paradigm. Therefore, if rationality and urban planning were weak in the face of power relations in Aalborg, then they were most likely weak everywhere else too. As his research unfolded, however, he soon realised that Aalborg was an 'extreme' case: both the rational planning paradigm *and* power relations were central to the case. So, in the face of this evidence, he changed his design and altered the way he reported the significance of his findings to his audience.

Simple enough, we might argue, and there is nothing here that is especially heretical from a naturalist perspective. Flyvbjerg simply dispensed with one hypothesis and created another. To be sure, his design no longer allowed him to falsify his initial hypothesis (and Flyvbjerg documents how this realisation was initially hard to swallow), but his extreme case could nevertheless reveal interesting exploratory insights that could be tested against a broader population or sample. There are several problems with this interpretation.

The first is contained in Flyvbjerg's admission that it took him months to come to terms with the fact that his material was not a 'critical' case because it undermined his ability to falsify his initial hypothesis. At the most basic level, the veneration of generalisability and predictability as the ultimate ends of social science makes it tempting for scholars to ignore inconvenient findings in order to maintain the integrity of the initial design. In the naturalist paradigm, this problem is significant. For an interpretive standpoint, this issue is less important because generalisability and predictability are not the main goals of research. In which case, there is no hierarchy of case selection strategies that a researcher can adopt. There are simply different ways of justifying or elucidating what it is about our research that makes it interesting.

The second more serious problem is that this reframing overlooks the fact that all data can be many types of cases *at the same time.* So, Flyvbjerg changed his case selection justification for the audience he wanted to address, but if he had changed his audience, he may well have been able to reconstruct his case as 'critical' for a different debate in a different literature. From a naturalist perspective, retrofitting hypotheses to match data is problematic because it undermines the scientific premise upon which his research was based (although we suspect it is a common practice). A new hypothesis means the researcher is conducting a new piece of research and essentially everything done prior becomes irrelevant or forgotten, with the researcher pretending they meant to investigate an extreme case all along.

Such methodological gymnastics are not required in interpretive research. Each case can always be many things to many audiences. The researcher is free to pick and choose which part of the story to tell depending on who their audience is. This is because findings are always partial, temporal and fleeting. To quote Wildavsky (2010: 13):

...the imposition of order on recalcitrant material which, we optimistically call knowledge, is a sometimes thing, hard-won, temporary, and artificial, like the rest of civilisation.

This humility about what we produce, and the freedom it provides, is indispensable because, as we will discuss in the next chapter, one of the greatest dangers in interpretive projects is that the researcher becomes so enmeshed in their data that they are unable to see the wood through the trees (see Chapter 5 on fieldwork). Recognising that findings do not have to be packaged in a single, coherent publication but different parts can instead be carved off for different audiences, and cases can be justified differently each time, is the key to unlocking the creative potential of interpretive research. When we enter the field, we will find many new and interesting things. Restricting ourselves to the research design we started with, or having to throw out prior knowledge when we change direction, just does not make sense, philosophically or pragmatically.

The ability to be flexible in how a case is justified is especially crucial for comparative interpretive projects. At the most basic level, as we will outline in Rule #7 below, this is because one of the easiest ways for researchers who do in-depth fieldwork to make their work explicitly comparative is to collaborate with other scholars. In such instances, it is highly likely that at least one of the collaborators will be justifying their case in an entirely different way to their initially designe. But, it is also because when deciding to compare, we choose cases specifically because they allow us to explore different aspects of the same phenomenon. Flyvbjerg changed his single case from 'critical' to 'extreme'. He could have also added cases and made his design primarily focused on elucidating differences between similar cases, or similarities between different cases, and in doing so altered the justification for his knowledge claims.

The important point is that these types of changes are not a product of faulty initial design or selection for the simple reason that the researchers could not have foreseen what they would discover in the field. Rather, they emerged from abductive immersion in theory and data. Adapting, revising, redesigning and retrospectively refitting data to different theories are a key sign that a project is taking shape and that the researcher, or team of researchers, is starting to open up and puzzle with the topic at hand.

Having dispelled the myth that changing cases is a bad idea, or that changing the way a case is justified is somehow antithetical to 'proper' social science, we turn to the more pragmatic question of how this stance affects design choices about case selection. Specifically, we dwell on when to think about making changes, and how to decide which way to go when in the middle of doing the research. The obvious point to start with here is that there are no clear-cut answers to these questions. All research, but particularly comparative interpretive research, is a messy and unpredictable business, in which hindsight is the only sure way of determining whether a choice was the right one. We do not cover decisions about data collection here because we will discuss that in Chapter 5. In general, we suggest following both your instincts and where you are led by your respondents.

Rule #5: Follow Where You Are Led; and Take What You Can Get

While it is important to trust ourselves when making these decisions, they do not need to be faced alone. We are not here referring to the support networks that surround any research project – peers and colleagues, supervisors and mentors – although obviously they can act as valuable sounding boards and provide sage advice. Rather, consistent with the interpretive commitment to treating participants as co-producers of knowledge, we can gain valuable insight into enlightening sources of comparison through listening attentively to what those in the field are saying. The comparisons that these actors draw – to other countries or regions, other controversies or conflicts, other organisations or practices – can emerge as the most fruitful to explore because they are in a unique position to compare the dilemmas they face to those faced by actors in another time or place.

Take Boswell's study of the debate around obesity policy. He began with a single case focused on the national debate in Australia. Initially, he justified it in accordance with emerging orthodoxies around single case research. In practice, he kept his options open to pursue a form of comparison. The key question was about whether to do, and what the optimal comparative case might be. He decided to take his cue from actors in the field. In their public advocacy and private reflections, he found more and more that actors typically reached for two analogies. One was the debate around tobacco control within Australia – that the debate around obesity in Australia paralleled (but lagged about 20 years behind) the debate around smoking. The other analogy was the obesity debate in the UK – that the debate in Australia was cruder and nastier than that in the UK. Both sets of comparison came up, unprompted, in nearly every interview. Both were often deeply personal. They emerged from health advocates who had fought the same fight against Big Tobacco 20 years prior, or were based on professional experience and overlap in the UK and Australia. Boswell increasingly viewed these organic modes of comparison not only as valuable data in their own right – as emerging patterns or themes in the field – but also as a source of guidance for complementary case analysis. He even moved to finishing his interviews by explicitly discussing potential avenues or sources of comparison for the study, with a particular focus on these two options.

Ideally, he would have pursued both cases as comparators, but time and resource constraints forced a pragmatic choice, one which brought back into focus fundamental questions of motivation. What was he trying to achieve? He was personally motivated by seeing obesity as a case of democratic debate on a wicked, irresolvable 'problem'. Indeed, for public health audiences, he would introduce himself as being perhaps the only person in the room not interested in solving the obesity issue. The dilemmas that interested him most were dilemmas around how actors ought to pursue advocacy and steer public debate. He realised any argument on this front would be easier to prosecute by expanding the geographical rather than issue focus. Strategically, though there might have been considerable mileage (and certainly a lot more grant money!) in pursuing a research career in the field of public health in Australia, his training and sense of identity was grounded in public policy and political science. Over time, he surmised that an Australian focus would be limiting for his career aspirations. Put simply, drawing comparison with the UK – a bigger, higher-profile country and one that a much larger pool of political scientists is intrinsically interested in – would be 'smart' for his chances of publishing and landing a job.

The point, then, is not that embracing co-production can absolve the responsibility of making key decisions about what cases to study. What it can do, however, is serve a valuable role in sharpening these choices by letting the data guide the choice of comparison. Working with, and listening to, participants in the field can narrow down and sift through whether to pursue avenues of comparison and, if so, which ones.

In sum, there is a rich vein of interpretive thinking about how what a piece of research is a case of can change over the life of the project. Comparative interpretive research only sharpens these questions as the more cases there are, the more ways there are to tell different stories to different audiences, including adding or abandoning cases, changing question or topic. The only rules of thumb are to follow your own intuition; 'go where you are led'; and 'take what you can get' (Fenno 1990: chapter 3). The process is often messy and unpredictable, and can lead to considerable anxiety, especially when going through the process for the first time. This reaction is normal. The fail-safe is that because interpretive research is about human beings and the dilemmas they confront in their everyday lives, there are always interesting stories to tell. While design choices can feel daunting, true dead ends are rare. The key challenge is deciding what the interesting story is and which audience will be most receptive to it.

After Data Collection

Rule #6: Remember the Project Never 'Ends'

When we embrace the comparative intuition, we can see new potential for re-imagining what our study is a case of. The way we teach and write about research design generally treats each project as a discrete piece of work like a PhD thesis. For most career academics, conducting discrete, tightly contained projects is rare. More often, we are working on multiple projects at once and the boundaries between them blur. This blurring can often feel overwhelming so the tendency is to try to draw artificial boundaries around what we do: for example, between our 'primary' and our 'side' projects. Such boundaries might be useful when interviewing for a job or writing a grant application because it gives our work the appearance of a coherent narrative. When seeking to embrace our comparative intuition, distinctions between projects and topics is less helpful. Drawing out unlikely affinities between disparate cases is often the best way to develop new ideas. No matter how eclectic our research interests, most of us will return to recurring themes and dilemmas, not only because they reflect our normative preferences and aspirations but also because there is often less variety beneath the surface of the human experience than we presume.

The easiest way for interpretivists to extend their comparative work is to augment an already completed project. Rhodes, Wanna and Weller's (2009) study compared executive government in five Westminster dominion states – Australia, Canada, New Zealand, South Africa and the UK. One of the core dilemmas was the supplementing, even supplanting, of the advice of public servants with advice from political appointees. Rhodes and Tiernan (2014) further explored this dilemma in their analysis of the changing role of chiefs of staff to Australian prime ministers. There is now a database of some 200 interviews that will form the base line for the next project. Past research informs new directions, adds new cases, updates material, adds new actors and facilitates comparison across time.

Rule #7: Collaborate to Increase the Number of Cases

Finding affinities between our research projects is useful, but if we are committed to doing the type of in-depth fieldwork that is often synonymous with interpretive research, then our opportunities for comparison are still likely to be limited by time and resources. A variation on the above strategy is therefore to collaborate with other scholars to realise the comparative potential of our research. The point is that the easiest way to add or reinvent a case, and in doing so overcome the depth-breadth trade-off in interpretive research (see Chapter 5), is to collaborate with other scholars who work on the same case but from a different perspective, or who work on a different case from a similar perspective (or both). Such collaboration involves embracing our intuition by engaging in constant comparison, seeking out and exploring affinities and discrepancies with the work of peers and colleagues.

Boswell's (2016a) work on the political debate surrounding obesity policy is a case in point. His initial project covered the politics of obesity in two countries, and aimed to speak mainly to public health and policy scholars. Subsequently, he collaborated with Ercan (2015) and Hendriks (2016), and their studies of the politics of 'honour killings' in Germany and sustainable energy policy in New South Wales, respectively, to speak to contemporary debates about public deliberation on complex and contested issues (see Boswell et al. 2016). As the authors' own programmes of work have evolved (see Boswell 2018; Ercan et al. 2017; Hendriks 2017), they have subsequently broadened the scope of cases and countries in a continuing collaborative project focused on understanding and addressing so-called 'democratic disconnects' in contemporary governance. No two of the cases are exactly alike. Each has its own idiosyncrasies in terms of substantive focus, guided by what has been interesting and important in the case at hand. Each relies on its own particular combination of data collection and methods of analysis, directed by what was possible in the field. But they share enough in common that makes comparison fruitful and sustains the collaboration.

An important point to draw from this example is that concern with sample size and representativeness should not be a major barrier to attempting these types of comparison. Often when attempting to combine material in a new project we worry about whether the data are comparable – i.e. whether the sample is sufficiently similar and representative. These considerations are important because the data need to be justified, but they can also be overstated. As both examples show, gaining the same number of interviews with the same types of actors has little relevance to either the methodological or practical aims of comparative interpretive research. None of the material is representative, and all such comparisons are necessarily partial. The key test is whether the authors collected enough material to convince their chosen audience they have uncovered all of the relevant perspectives. When in doubt, follow the conventions of similar studies in the field to which the study contributes.

In sum, all interpretive research is open-ended and constantly evolving. There is the potential to adapt, revise, redesign and retrospectively refit our projects after we have collected the data. This flexibility is true of explicitly comparative projects. However, it applies also to single case studies, which we can augment either by further research, or by collaborations, to draw out their comparative potential. One of the main barriers to such comparisons is the perception they are hard to justify methodologically. In a strict naturalist paradigm that may well be true. However, interpretivists have greater freedom in the way they justify what and how they study. As we will discuss further in Chapter 7, this is as much about function of presentation and communication as it is about design.

Conclusion

The social science ideal is that research design and case selection is determined at the beginning of the project in order to test hypothesis derived from the theoretical literature. Interpretive research works on different assumptions. It is not entirely inductive – i.e. grounded theory (Glaser and Strauss 2017 [1967]) – but rather abductive in nature, involving an iterative interaction between theory and practice. As a result, *what* we study and *how* we study it are constantly changing over the course of a research project to reflect new and emerging insights gained from immersion in our data. To guide this typically messy and chaotic process we identified three broad strategies – provisional, adaptive and reflective – and seven rules of thumb that are relevant to different stages of the research process.

Running through each rule of thumb is a commitment to being reflexive about the normative preferences of the researcher. From a methodological standpoint, as outlined in Chapter 2, interpretivists aspire to conduct *decentred* analysis. Each researcher will also have personal normative preferences for their project. We cannot control these preferences, or what naturalists call biases, nor would we want to control them! They represent our unique voice in the research project and thus are central to the value of what we do. The audience for our work does not only want to know what the actors in our stories do and say, but also how the author makes sense of their talk and practice. Deciding what to study, and how to study it, are both the first and last step in this endeavour, and, as we will outline in the following chapters, it informs all of the stages in between.

5 Fieldwork

Corbett delivered his PhD confirmation seminar paper – a rite of passage before being allowed out into the field – to a mix of awe, bewilderment and scepticism from the eclectic audience at his home institution. There was broad agreement that he had uncovered an interesting and important gap in the field, as political leadership in the Pacific Islands remained relatively unexplored. He had a thorough theoretical grounding for the research, and he seemed to have a sound understanding of his proposed methodology. But did he think it would be possible to do fieldwork across the *whole region*? For the committed area specialists in the room the approach was highly dubious. Many had devoted their whole careers to just one Pacific state, or sometimes just one small region within one state. How exactly did Corbett think he was going to do in-depth fieldwork across fourteen countries?

In this chapter, we hope to show that this scepticism is both unfounded and limiting. It is possible to do in-depth and valuable fieldwork across multiple sites. In fact, Kapiszewski, Maclean and Read (2015: chapter 3) implicitly acknowledge that most scholars already work in multiple field sites, whether in the same country or region, or between types of data. However, the implications of such comparisons are seldom canvassed, apart from brief discussions of the breadth-depth trade-off. The question of how to compare remains mysterious. Schwartz-Shea and Yanow (2012) implicitly presume that interpretive research will favour depth over breadth. So, much of their discussion revolves around the relationship between the researcher and their data (cf. Yanow 2014). In this chapter, comparison is front and centre. The aim is not just to tell readers about how comparative fieldwork presents particular challenges and opportunities but also to show how we overcome challenges and maximise opportunities to produce richly detailed but theoretically significant research.

To achieve the multiple aims of comparative interpretive fieldwork – to provide a decentred account by comparing dilemmas across contexts – we need to draw on multiple methods of data collection. As we have outlined above, data for a comparative interpretive project may be qualitative or quantitative. It may come from participant observation, archival sources or interviews. We prefer qualitative data in our work, and so much of this chapter will be devoted to this type of fieldwork. But, we are philosophically committed to using whatever data are suitable to a particular study, and to mixing and matching different forms of data to tell each story in the most arresting, evocative or interesting way. In short, we see fieldwork as a diverse set of practices, and we refer to ourselves as *bricoleurs*, or Jacks-and-Jills-of-all-trades, gathering material when, where and how we can (Levi-Strauss 1966: 16–17).

Seeing the Wood through the Trees

The reason we are flexible about the types of data we use is that all empirical research ultimately must serve a broader argument. For many scholars who work in the naturalist tradition, fieldwork suffers from a series of shortcomings, especially the inability to generalise from a single or few cases; unsystematic evidence; and biased respondents. However, as we explained at some length in Chapter 2, interpretive researchers reject these negative characterisations of fieldwork and the principles that underpin them. Nonetheless, interpretive researchers can fall foul of fieldwork's most common pitfall – not being able to see the theoretical wood through the empirical trees. As a result, they are more liable to focus on rich idiographic detail but lose sight of broader theoretical issues.

We say wood *through* the trees rather than wood *for* the trees because the term *through* suggests that interpretivist researchers make knowledge claims only after passing *through* their fieldwork data. The great and common danger for interpretivists, especially among PhD students but not exclusively so, is that they never make it *through* their data. Instead of mining their material for interesting themes, they remain mired in an ever-deepening pool of detail. The tell-tale sign is the seminar, conference paper or even book that is full of interesting substance but the point, if there is one, is far from clear. We plead guilty. We too have become fascinated by the detail at the expense of plausible conjectures. There is an unavoidable trade-off between the depth central to the humanist endeavour and the breadth required to make general statements. This chapter is a guide on how to pass *through* fieldwork with something interesting to say at the end.

There are also new and often unfamiliar questions in comparative interpretive research. How to prepare for multiple field settings, and where to start?

How to approach the field in and across each of these settings? How much data to collect and when to stop in each case? How to 'capture' adequately each field? Does such an inquiry fit with the 'lone wolf' image so central to the humanist tradition? How to cope given the upheaval entailed in moving across sites?

The Rules of Thumb for Fieldwork

The rest of this chapter provides some 'rules of thumb' that will guide researchers as they go about seeking answers to these questions. Table 5.1 lists the rules. This approach is not unique; others also emphasise flexibility in much the way we do (see, for example, Kapiszewski, Maclean and Read 2015).

Rule #1: Be Pragmatic and Opportunistic

Where to start? The most common rule of thumb for undertaking empirical research is the research design model we were all exposed to as graduate students – literature review, theoretical approach, case selection, data collection, data analysis and writing-up. As outlined in the previous chapter, we are not enamoured with this step-by-step process. But we do agree that the sequence in which data are collected is important, not only for the success of the project but also because it frames the questions we ask and what we find.

In naturalist mode, sequencing is vital for the validity of fieldwork data. The particular concern is to ensure reliability and eliminate any potential bias, understood as a comparability or symmetry in data sources and data collection. Timing, then, is important. Fieldwork in this tradition is planned down to the fine detail. There are sequenced phases; for example, from pilot

Table 5.1 Rules of thumb for fieldwork

1. Be pragmatic and opportunistic
2. Start writing straight away
3. Yo-yo in and out of field sites
4. Make interviews everyday conversations; choose and play your parts in them purposefully
5. Expose findings to a broad array of voices and search for a fusion of horizons
6. Collaborate when you can
7. Learn how to muddle through

study to full study. The aim is to control for confounding variations that might be introduced by a different sequence; for example, lapses in time between visits to comparative sites. The problem with this search for control is that the field is typically much messier than any step-by-step plan can possibly account for. Such an approach is poorly equipped not only to deal with the inevitable setbacks that occur, but also to capitalise on important opportunities that arise.

The humanist tradition, by contrast, revels in the haphazard and unexpected happenings of the field. In PhD research, coping with what the field throws up – including changing the focus of research inquiry – is a defining rite of passage. The idea is not to control for deviation but to dwell on it and follow where it leads. Typically, sequencing is presented as unimportant to the humanist tradition. Where we start and finish hardly matters. The key is in the experience of the journey, not the destination. Researchers should 'follow their nose', 'go where they are led' and 'take what you can get' (Fenno 1990: chapter 3).

For comparative research the traditional 'voyage of discovery' when writ large in the way practitioners typically imagine it, might be unattainable. It depends on factors that are scarce in comparative research: time and money. The long sojourn that has historically defined the humanist 'soak' in the field is a key ingredient in gaining a host of important fieldwork resources and attributes. It enables the slow build-up of language skills, local knowledge and understanding of norms and customs that is typically central to interpretive research. It also allows the researcher to build networks and gain access to important sites, practices and individuals. The challenge of comparative interpretive research thus becomes obvious, with Corbett's (2015a) study being an extreme example.

Fieldwork in the Pacific region – still a stronghold of humanist anthropology – typically entails intensive immersion in a single urban or rural setting. Corbett's research took in fourteen countries. So, how can comparative interpretive research of this sort achieve rich nuance and understanding, and attain the necessary access, in much shorter periods? When deep immersion is not practical, the solution lies in yo-yoing in and out of multiple sites – see Rule #3. Sociologists have long practised such 'partial immersion' (Delamont 2007: 206). The researcher is a *bricoleur* who chooses research tools and the duration of any field trip. The point of starting with pragmatic considerations is to emphasise that there is no ideal way to do fieldwork and no essential data to collect. But there are better and worse ways to do the fieldwork for any particular project. Thinking through the pragmatic considerations can help to avoid making fieldwork harder than it needs to be. The comparative interpretive focus on dilemmas can serve to shape and drive these pragmatic choices.

The key fact here is that some dilemmas that interest social scientists will recur more or less predictably across settings, while others will emerge or fall away on closer inspection. Early forays into the field can centre on getting a broad overview, probing only more deeply into predictable and recurring dilemmas in the initial stages. The researcher dips in and out at strategic points, opportunistically accumulating insights and puzzling further and deeper. This necessitates a degree of *flexible planning.* Time in the field is a precious resource that requires specific targeting, but the researcher must remain open to exploring new options and taking advantage of new opportunities as they arise.

So how might such probing begin? We are advocates of Hajer's (1996) 'helicopter' approach – begin with three or four actors ('helicopters') who are chosen because they have the overview of the field from different vantage points. For example, when interviewing ministers and public servants in Denmark and the Netherlands, Rhodes also talked to the political correspondents of the local broadsheet newspapers. They were not interviews. Rhodes sought their advice on whom to talk to, and solicited introductions. He was given a steer on what to talk about in later interviews. It also allowed him to preface questions with 'others have told me', which helped to ensure that the discussion proceeded as a non-threatening conversation rather than an inquisition. Other examples of helicopter interviews might include retired politicians, a key advisor to the government or an expert on a specific policy area. Helicopter conversations are only a starting point. They have their limits. For any journalist, information is power or, at least, the next byline. So they can be cagey about sharing. They are reassured when told it will be three years before the book comes out. Three years is a lifetime for a journalist. They may not be dead, but all of today's stories are well and truly buried.

The other key issue about planning and sequencing is opportunism – a willingness to tweak plans or follow up on opportunities that can save on time and associated resources. Once again, alertness towards such opportunities can be guided by the focus on dilemmas, and expectations about which dilemmas are likely to recur. In particular, because he was working across fourteen countries, Corbett (2015a) targeted large international meetings where he knew numerous politicians from different countries would be present. Such events provided him with not only an opportunity to interview politicians from across his fourteen countries but also to engage with them during and after the event in more informal ways. The payoff was two-fold. One was simply that he collected much data in a relatively short time. Also, he built new networks through which to secure access to further participants. What would have taken him months to achieve in-country was done and dusted in a few days. The other benefit was that it was a shortcut to sorting and sifting similarities and differences in experiences, practices and beliefs across the region. Indeed, in these informal conversations, to which we return in Rule #4, politicians often began to associate their experiences with the experiences of others. In effect, they started doing his comparisons for him.

The field can be overwhelming and throw up surprises for even the well-prepared researcher with the most considered research design. Such uncertainty applies to comparative projects where time in the field is more precious, making the stakes higher. The understandable temptation is therefore to prepare and design comparative projects better in the hope of controlling for the unexpected. Our approach is different: we consciously seek out the unexpected. Indeed, we argue there is little reason to go into the field if one does not hope to encounter ways of seeing and acting in the world that we do not immediately understand. One can anticipate some of the dilemmas that actors confront. We are unlikely to anticipate how they attempt to solve them, and the impact of their actions, without spending time with them. Our aim is to embolden researchers to embrace the field and its uncertainties. The key to coping is the writing.

Rule #2: Start Writing Straight Away

The typical research design expects that writing will come *after* fieldwork and analysis. We have found that the two are intermingled – a point especially true for comparative projects where the 'field' involves multiple sites. If the key question is 'what is similar or different' (see Chapter 4), then it is imperative the researcher has some idea of what they have found in their first field site before they enter the second. Such advice might sound obvious, but it flies in the face of the naturalist concern with eliminating bias. In the conventional rendering, the researcher should avoid making judgements about their existing data to ensure their impressions do not influence how they experience the next field site. We disagree. It is impossible to 'control' for our impressions in this way (Boswell and Corbett 2015a). If we are doing the fieldwork ourselves, then our brains will naturally form patterns even if we have not written anything down. More importantly, it denies the researcher their most crucial advantage when entering the field: their ability to be surprised and thus shift focus and direction. As we pointed out in Chapter 1, we describe this process as *puzzling* to capture its iterative quality.

The humanist tradition is typically much more receptive to open-ended inquiry. In fact, for the demands of comparative interpretive research, we think it is *too* open-ended. The taboo about writing-up too early, in this sense, is something that naturalists and humanist social sciences typically share. But where naturalists are concerned about bias, humanists are mainly concerned about closing off potential avenues of inquiry and capturing, and crystallising around, a stylised or limited understanding. So, researchers should hold off from writing until they have suffered sufficiently long bouts of dwelling in their data – enough time to reach the 'Eureka!' moment of clarity that somehow 'captures' the subject in question (see Boswell and Corbett 2015a).

The dichotomy between the two orthodoxies is perhaps best illustrated by Kvale and Brinkmann's (2009) influential distinction between the interviewer as a traveller, on a voyage of discovery, and the interviewer as a miner, seeking specific information (see also Kapiszewski, Maclean and Read (2015) on 'flexible discipline'). Our argument is that all researchers must perform both roles in the field. Once again, the central focus on dilemmas shapes the appropriate orientation at any given time. In any comparative interpretive project, some dilemmas identified in the field will recur across settings, while others will emerge only in a specific tradition in a particular setting. The orientation of the researcher shifts as these similarities and differences become apparent. The traveller, then, is more common in the early stages of the fieldwork. The aim is to ascertain what dilemmas actors perceive and experience, which ones travel, which are context-bound. Here, everything should be new and interesting. Later, the miner comes into play as the research gets an overarching sense of the range of dilemmas, and the extent of their resonance across settings. As fieldwork progresses, data collection becomes more directed at specific gaps in understanding. But it is not a steady or linear progression. Surprising changes, unexpected insights or new moments of analytical inspiration can tilt the researcher back and forth between orientations. The *bricoleur* will adapt the research strategy and adopt any relevant tools to understand a surprise.

For Rhodes, in his ethnographic comparison of government departments at Whitehall, writing in a fieldwork notebook enabled him to make sense of his observations. The fieldwork notebook is the most striking fieldwork practice of ethnographers for a political scientist (see Bryman 2001: vol. 2, part 7; Charmaz 2006; Emerson, Fretz and Shaw 2011; Sanjek 1990). It is simultaneously invisible and ever-present, part of the tacit knowledge of fieldworkers. It serves two functions. First, for Rhodes, it was a source of evidence. He found it useful for comparing the data he collected with statements made in interviews. He could explore contradictions in further interviews and through more observation. Second, it was a mechanism for coping with the emotional and other stresses and strains of fieldwork (see Rule #7 below). Here, we focus on writing-up fieldwork observations as a process of gathering, and beginning to interpret, evidence.

Rhodes learnt to compile fieldwork notes on the job. There is no agreed definition of a fieldwork notebook, but some minimal order is necessary no matter what type of data is collected. Rhodes focused on collecting observational data, and he kept the data in time and date order. 'Observation' is a broad category, covering everyday activities, conversations, pen portraits of individuals and new ideas about how to do the research. Therefore, the following example is not typical or ideal. It is one fieldworker's experience of the fieldwork notebook as evidence.

On each visit to a department, Rhodes described the physical space, the decor and the appearance of the people under observation. He made jottings on the run and compiled more substantial notes at the end of the working day. He presented himself as just another note taking committee clerk, even if a tad old. Note taking was selective. It was straightforward to record what was significant for the observed; often they would tell him what they thought important. Sometimes he was asked not to take notes. Afterwards, he would pop into the toilet to make notes before they faded from memory. Most of the time we are on our own, and there is far more to record than can be recorded. Rhodes developed the habit of writing on only one side of paper so, when reviewing notes later that night, he could add further observations from memory on the back of the page.

He would check the data collected if only because, on occasion, he could not understand his record. He used the reverse of the pages in his notebook to unpack an acronym or record the prior history of an event. He would talk to people again to clarify the notes and his understanding of them. Informal conversations and pen portraits of people rounded out interviews. Interviews and documents were cross-referenced to the notebooks to provide context for both. With the interviews and documentary sources, the notebooks provided essential data for final analysis. Rhodes' interpretations would change as he learnt more. Indeed, it was interpretation all the way down and some puzzles were not 'resolved' until the final writing-up. When used to collect data, we do not claim the notebooks were 'objective' or 'authoritative'. If the aim is to treat the notebooks as evidence, then being clear about the aim and purpose is essential.

A more radical departure from the humanist orthodoxy is to start writing-up insights from the field into formal academic prose. Naturally, much of this initial drafting will end up on the cutting room floor. It might lack fine-grained accuracy, suppress nuance or reach hasty interpretations. Nevertheless, we have found the practice of writing-up 'as if' finished – typically to share with collaborators and mentors, or present to conference audiences – a vital crutch in complex comparative work. It helps us sharpen what is unique about the comparative insights we are gaining and clarify gaps in our understanding.

Again Corbett (2015a) provides a relevant example. Having analysed all of the autobiographies/biographies in the 'helicopter' phase of the project, he started writing-up his key themes and found he had a solid enough grasp of the pathways in and through politics in the Pacific Islands for a full paper based on this publicly available data. As he set off to the field, he submitted the paper to a peer–reviewed journal where it was published eventually (see Corbett 2012). Obviously, this outcome provided a welcome confidence boost for a young researcher still early in his PhD journey. It was also instrumentally useful in today's 'publish or perish' academic culture. But, more unexpectedly, he also benefited from the *process* of formally writing-up this initial analysis, especially the feedback provided via peer review, rather than just its happy outcome. He found it extremely useful in pushing along his thinking on the topic. Specifically, it enabled him to settle his research questions and begin identifying answers to them in the surprising commonalities they revealed across contexts. Inevitably, in going into the field he uncovered many subtle differences in the nature and depth of these initial findings across the countries in his analysis – the sort of findings that can only come from intensive fieldwork. These richer insights are reflected in the greater complexities and nuances of the more truly 'finished' product, his later book-length treatment (see Corbett 2015a). But the earlier commitment to writing-up – even if it had not been in published form – had played an instrumental role in driving the project along.

We do not ignore the often expressed fears about 'biasing' interpretation. Such cautions are wise. Would Corbett have found something different had he not already analysed and written about the autobiographies/biographies?

Highly likely! Were certain avenues of inquiry inadvertently closed off in the process? Almost certainly! The point is that, as with the above discussion of sequencing, any defensible approach to fieldwork would come with its own set of biases (related, for instance, to material gathered most recently) or would inevitably close down possible avenues of inquiry (related, for instance, to sticky themes developed through writing in a fieldwork notebook). These limitations and foibles are inevitable. All a researcher can do is be reflexive about it in their study (see Corbett 2015a: 17). Moreover, any apparent trade-off was, he felt, well worth it. Indeed, it was only by approaching the field as an active writer, rather than passive observer, that he was able to play the part of *bricoleur*, moving effectively between 'miner' and 'traveller' orientations to gain the breadth and depth of insight his ambitious project required.

Rule #3: Yo-yo In and Out of Field Sites

The rule of thumb that most academics live by when it comes to data is: the more the better. In this section, we want to push back against this characterisation. There is no magic number for how long to spend in the field. There is no magic number for the interviews that need to be conducted or documents read. Most importantly, more is manifestly not always better. Indeed, in our experience more exacerbates the proverbial wood through the trees problem as often as it leads to richer and deeper insights. 'More is better' is also an impossible standard for comparativists because there is a pragmatic trade-off to be made between depth and breadth.

It is tempting to claim that the 'more is better' ideal is the result of the growth of quantitative political science. But in truth more avowedly humanist disciplines, such as anthropology, have been peddling this line for some time, with Malinowski's extended stay in the Trobriand Islands the gold standard. Although the appropriateness of Malinowski's deep hanging out style of fieldwork has been challenged in anthropology (for example, Clifford 1986), many scholars in this field remain sceptical of anything less than a year's fieldwork. At the area studies school where Corbett did his PhD training, it was common for anthropologists to list the number of months they had spent in the field on their CVs just as political scientists list the methods courses they have undertaken or the software packages they have mastered. It is difficult to imagine a better example of 'more is better' thinking.

The avowed strength of the 'more is better' approach to fieldwork is that it allows the scholar to claim a rich and detailed engagement with their data.

They appreciate the nuances and the subtleties. They know the history and, where necessary, the language. Commonly, however, we posit that the real reason scholars are encouraged to collect more and more data is that it is the easiest way to lay claim to an original contribution. In turn, bigger datasets assuage researcher anxiety about producing relevant findings. Indeed, if the dataset is perceived as big enough, then the researcher may never have to worry about finding a way through the trees: they can simply fall back on 'well my data says' when faced with even the most minor criticism. Deep hanging out Malinowski-style has its place in political science. But it has numerous drawbacks. The most obvious is that the findings, while rich and subtle, can be idiographic. It can also compound the perfectionist anxieties associated with the impossible need to produce a definitive magnum opus which 'somehow captures' everything.

The alternative norm in naturalist fieldwork is not so much that 'more is better' but instead the goal of representativeness. Applied to a research project like Corbett's, this would mean a statistically representative geographical spread from the relevant countries, plus other key descriptive characteristics such as age, gender, ethnicity and religion. The researcher would aim to gather responses across these categories and use them as variables on which to base their explanations of similarities and differences.

Underlying both sets of norms is the question of robustness, and the degree to which claims based on the fieldwork can be taken seriously. A lingering concern about the critical reception of their work can push researchers towards gathering more data than they need, and to making sure they achieve the appearance of a descriptively representative sample. Corbett (2014), for instance, reflects on how he kept gathering data in pursuit of a magic number of 100 interviews. He sought after a descriptive diversity of participants even though new interviews were yielding fewer and fewer insights. The ghosts of both naturalist and humanist orthodoxies can haunt researchers.

From a comparative interpretive perspective, more data is not necessarily a bad result – particularly if, as in Corbett's case, there is sufficient time and resource to pursue this additional face-saving field research. But such extra work buttresses neither total immersion nor statistical representativeness. Instead, it merely further elaborates complex specificity. If comparing the dilemmas that actors face across different contexts is at the heart of comparative interpretive research, then the task of fieldwork is to uncover the repertoire of responses to these dilemmas. Total immersion or a perfectly representative sample can achieve these ends, but at considerable cost in time and effort. The pragmatic obstacles to comparative interpretive research often require a shortcut.

But, if an extended stay is not practical, and the pursuit of representativeness artificial, then what will capture the diversity (common features and differences) between (say) states? What will sustain a creative abductive engagement with the theoretical literature? We argue that a more suitable approach in comparative interpretive research is what Wulff (2002) calls 'yo-yo' fieldwork and Geertz (2001: 141) 'hit and run ethnography'. So, we move in and out of the field, shifting between different sites, actors and data. Yo-yoing is how most scholars do fieldwork (Kapiszewski, Maclean and Read 2015: 59). In effect, we are simply giving a name to and a rationale for, current practices (see Geuijen, 't Hart and Yesilkagit 2007: 132 for an example of yo-yoing in and out of EU institutions). But the implication of explicitly embracing yo-yoing is potentially much greater than a new label. The point is that consciously and deliberately yo-yoing can allow researchers to maximise the strengths of this approach rather than treat it as a poor substitute for the real ('more is better') thing. The experience of yo-yoing forces the researcher to make sense of what is recurring and what is context specific in the way actors experience and respond to dilemmas. It also enables them to reflect on when they have enough data from a field site or when they need to go back for more.

To parse out what yo-yoing looks like let us again use Corbett (2015a) as an example. Corbett visited eleven of the fourteen countries in his study between 2011 and 2014 (he did the interviews for the other countries at international meetings in Australia, New Zealand and Tonga). The longest trip was his first: five weeks in Samoa during an election campaign. The shortest was a 48-hour stopover in the Federated States of Micronesia during which time he interviewed the sitting president, two former presidents and the senior senator. Perversely, he spent longer in all other field sites without getting even close to equivalent access. He returned to some countries (Fiji and Samoa) more than once. As well as interviews, he spent time working on a candidates' election campaign (Samoa), went to constituency meetings (Marshall Islands and Kiribati), attended parliament (Kiribati), donor meetings (Tonga) and regional forums (Palau). He went to funerals (Tuvalu), church services (Kiribati) and other community meetings (Marshall Islands) with politicians. He spent many hours interviewing in hotel restaurants and bars – both places where politicians do much of their work. Sometimes, he chose to stay in hotels because he knew they were owned by a particular politician and therefore would increase his access (and it worked). He spent countless hours waiting in ministerial offices or at businesses and homes, which gave him a good sense of how they operate and the part they play in a politicians' workday. He accepted a ride whenever offered, which produced some of the best material he collected. On occasions, he was invited to the home of a politician whom he had interviewed for a meal.

How much time did all of this add up to? Maybe a month or so of 'observation', combined with five or six more months in-country trying to organise interviews. It was not long enough for anthropologists to put it on their CV. But well within the established conventions of yo-yoing fieldwork in political science (for example, Fenno 1978; Rhodes 2011). Corbett does not claim to 'have seen the world as they see it', but he is comfortable with the idea that he saw 'some of their world' (see also Reeher 2006). The observation experience added depth and richness to the account obtained via interviews and other public sources. But, more importantly, what it enabled him to do was challenge the common presumption among area studies scholars in the Pacific that these countries could not be compared in the way he proposed. Not only were Corbett's politicians similar to one another, but their job was in many ways remarkably similar to the job in larger and richer democracies (for example, Reeher (2006) in the USA). In this way, yo-yoing enabled Corbett to capture not only what is different about each country but also what is shared by politicians everywhere. He could have spent more time in each of these field sites but he had already got more than he needed.

Rule #4: Make Interviews Everyday Conversations; Choose and Play Your Parts in Them Purposefully

The most common tool in qualitative social science is the interview and in political science, the elite interview. The most common format is a recorded, one-hour conversation around a semi-structured questionnaire (see, for example, Dexter 2006). Of course, it can be revealing in the hands of a skilled interviewer, but it courts the danger of becoming a confining ritual. All elite interviewers know the bureaucrat or politician who can negotiate such an encounter with ease and 'talk for an hour without saying anything too interesting' (Rawnsley 2001: xvii–xviii citing Robin Cooke, former British Foreign Secretary).

Rhodes' elites were bright, personable and fluent. One senior public servant gave him an ostensibly entertaining and informative interview, and he came out of the office thinking she was forthcoming and outgoing; it had been a good interview. He was confident there would be gems on the tape.

But when he read the transcript, it said almost nothing, though she said her 'nothings' in an entertaining fashion. These 'ritual' interviews are not helpful; it is hard to get behind the public facade. Politicians are skilled in interviews because they are doing them all the time, often faced with forensic, even aggressive, media interviewers. This problem can be acute in the context of comparative fieldwork where time is pressed, and capacity to obtain repeat interviews or additional interviewees may be restricted.

In short, the political science conception of an elite interview can be too narrow. There are other choices besides this format – the repeat interviews of ethnographic fieldwork and everyday conversations of an interpretive approach. The 'trick' is to persuade the interviewee to speak in a casual, informal way; to turn the encounter into an opportunity for the participant to unload or unburden themselves. These interviews never end. You both lose track of time. If there was a questionnaire, it has been long discarded. The goal is friendly conversations albeit conversations with an explicit purpose that take place either in the formal surroundings of the office or in the informal surroundings of a bar or hotel. We have found actors to be more open in such extended encounters because, as Rawnsley (2001: xi) observes, 'they have to tell an outsider because they are so worried about whether it makes sense or, indeed, whether they make sense'. But, we accept that encouraging informality in an interview is a craft, and this skill must be developed through practice (Fujii 2017; Weiss 1995).

Sometimes, with especially important informants, this might be achieved only by the repeat ethnographic interviews associated with the idiographic tradition. Rhodes' (2011) favourite interview started as the conventional one hour with a high-ranking official. He was pleasant, but the interview was an inconsequential chat. The official said that he had 'quite enjoyed' the interview, suggested Rhodes came back and gave him a date. When they did meet again, the official began by taking his jacket off and lying down on the settee. After about twenty minutes of talking, he got up, went to the cabinet and poured himself a glass of whisky. He came back, sat down and started sipping his whisky. He took his shoes off, then his tie. In the end, the conversation lasted four hours. No one can maintain a public facade for so long, and he did not even try.

However, there are other shortcuts if the pragmatic challenges of comparative fieldwork mitigate against the repeat interview strategy. A particularly useful shortcut is building a personal and professional network. For financial and domestic reasons, Boswell had significant practical limitations on fieldwork travel during his project on the comparative politics of obesity. He could conduct repeat interviews and meet informally with participants in Canberra, where he lived, but fieldwork trips elsewhere in Australia and to the UK had to be squeezed into tight windows. So, he drew on the strong rapport he had built up with Canberra-based informants to get inside the tight-knit national and transnational networks of public health officials, experts and advocates. He joined mailing lists, linked in on social media, attended workshops and requested direct personal introductions. He could therefore present himself as an 'insider'; a known quantity to participants on his tightly scheduled field trips. He could establish quickly a relaxed rapport. For example, one such interview participant greeted him as an old friend. She invited him in to her home, and standing in the kitchen over a cup of tea, launched into an hour-long, free-form monologue. She gave him the most important and insightful data obtained during the project before he had even asked a question.

Usually, though, such interviews are still a negotiation. Their success depends on intangibles like trust, rapport and empathy. With trust comes far more information than can be obtained from working through a semi-structured questionnaire. But winning that trust requires more than academic skills. It requires interpersonal skills that, at times, verge on acting. Interviewing cross nationally, but even in our native tongue, poses distinctive challenges. We have conducted most of our interviews in English, but it is a language with many disparate dialects. Local norms call for empathy and adjustment to the presentation of self. It is plausible that Rhodes dressed in black suit and addressed as professor can conduct a conversation as between equals with a senior public servant. It is not plausible for the PhD student who will be cast more in the role of supplicant. Conversely, Rhodes in black suit and addressed as professor may fare less well than the casually dressed PhD when talking to street-level bureaucrats. Rhodes could all too easily be associated with 'management' or other group in positions of authority. The point is know the audience, dress in context, and choose and play the appropriate part with conviction.

Finally, lest we be accused of underestimating the skills of our academic colleagues, any fieldworker worth his or her salt will use any and all ways of interviewing. We do. Our point is to encourage fieldworkers where possible to aim for more than the standard one-hour ritual.

Rule #5: Expose Findings to a Broad Array of Voices and Search for a Fusion of Horizons

Perhaps the crucial part of the calculus in determining when to stop doing fieldwork is knowing when the story is 'right'. We consciously place the term in inverted commas because reflexivity about the provisional and contingent nature of research findings is central to interpretive research. The findings of comparative interpretive research are even more contingent because of its broader sweep and bolder theoretical ambitions. Yet it still captures the doubt that pervades fieldwork. We search for reassurance that our account is sufficiently authentic and nuanced, and that the insights we develop will encourage participants and scholars to engage in earnest and respectful reflection.

However, we share the interpretive critique of any science of storytelling that '"Truth" has become "truth": multifaceted, theoretically loaded, and embedded in historically situated language games and ordinary practice' (Wagenaar 2016: 134). There is no singular truth claim about complex social phenomena. Indeed, one of the most painful side effects of conducting fieldwork is awareness of the full complexities. Analysis can never do full justice to the outliers and exceptions, the lingering uncertainties and the unexplained, and the alternative explanations and unknowns.

Interpretivists are still concerned with getting the story 'right', but the means by which they examine their claims are different from those of naturalist colleagues. Rather than prediction and replicability, the most crucial test for interpretivists is whether their portrayal resonates with the people who are the subjects of the research. Indeed, the importance of co-production is why there is such intense debate among interpretivists about the right label for the participants in any research project (for discussion see Hendriks 2007). Naturalists are typically wary of such approaches in that they are seen to bias findings, 'rubber stamping' the analyst's hypothesis rather than objectively testing it. Obviously, given all we have said so far, we demur. We see great value in the practices of co-production – getting participants to reflect on and engage with emerging findings is essential in challenging some ideas and adding layers of nuance to others. Triangulation in the naturalist tradition implies a certainty that does not exist. Equally, co-production in idiographic research implies the possibility of a shared interpretation.

Comparative interpretive research depends on many voices and the search for a fusion of horizons. It is an attempt to capture and portray authentically a social context in full awareness of the shifting meanings, evolving practices and competing interpretations that surround it. The dilemmas at the centre of comparative interpretive analysis are of course themselves not stable and fixed, but fluid and open to different interpretations. The researcher's role in identifying them externally imposes a fixedness that makes comparative analysis feasible, and we think fruitful. But the commitment to reflexivity requires maintaining an awareness of this interpretive role (see Hay 2011), and being open to the prospect of reconsidering and revising the analysis. Incorporating many voices entails exposing emerging findings to an increasingly broad array of sources. It means being willing to engage in practices akin to triangulation, piecing together different sources to flesh out findings and identify disjuncture between beliefs and practices. But it also means engaging in practices of co-production by sharing emerging insights with research participants and encouraging their active engagement in interpreting the data. So, when the data in interviews contradict our observations, we ask the participants about the discrepancy and explore it with them. We do not expect a fusion of horizons from every encounter. It is our ambition but not always the practice. But when we disagree, we aim to seek further clarification. We expect our respondents at least to recognise themselves in our story and have some insight into what we have to say, even if they do not agree with our final interpretation. The final account is our account. It is our judgement about the weight of the evidence (for discussion, see Hay 2017).

Such findings are always provisional, and fieldwork is open-ended. Nevertheless, it is enough that the contingent findings are nuanced, interesting and plausible, and that interpretive decisions are discussed reflexively and justified explicitly. Most notably, there are always going to be exceptions. Not all material fits into the neat categories that researchers create in conversation with their data. The question is how to account for these exceptions when doing fieldwork. Rather than controlling for dissenting voices, or seeking to determine the 'true' version of the story using triangulation, interpretivists seek to place dissenting accounts side by side with the more orthodox narrative(s) that emerge from the field. But, it can also make sense to exclude exceptions altogether. Indeed, in a comparative project, it can become apparent that a specific case, which appeared well suited to the study in the beginning, ends up fitting awkwardly. For example, Corbett's project focused on the Pacific region. But the region has no fixed boundary. He started with the fourteen independent and self-governing political entities. As his fieldwork progressed he puzzled about how things might be similar and different in other parts of the region. For example, how different were politicians in Hawaii or Guam, or Pacific Islanders in the New Zealand parliament? So, he decided to interview a few of each to find out what was similar and what was different. He found that while the dilemmas were similar, the practices were different. His explanation was that political life in these larger jurisdictions was much more professionalised – full time, highly paid, well resourced – than in his original fourteen cases. Corbett could have incorporated this difference into his study, but he felt it would have dominated it: the distinction between 'professional' and 'amateur' politics would become the overriding theme. So, instead he decided to delimit the study to the fourteen countries in his initial plan (for discussion see Corbett 2015a: 12–16). But, such puzzling helped him clarify the practices that were unique to the countries he was looking at. It made him more confident in claiming the dilemmas he had uncovered had relevance beyond the Pacific. It provided the basis for later articles that either probed the professionalisation question in more detail (Corbett 2014), or included the additional material (Corbett and Liki 2015).

As his fieldwork progressed, Corbett (2015a) sent draft chapters to willing interviewees. The strategy bore fruit because the interviewees pinpointed disagreements. He would then amend the text to reflect these nuances. But, because politicians had a limited understanding of the practice of politics in different countries, their singular reflections were of limited use for the comparative side of his research (they were much better at identifying these when discussing in a group). Indeed, most remained sceptical that such a comparison was possible, a point he acknowledges in the book (Corbett 2015a: 23). Rhodes (2011: 302–305) had a different experience – see the account in Chapter 7.

Rule #6: Collaborate When You Can

The typical research design text imagines a single researcher heroically collecting and mining a plethora of data to produce significant findings. This ideal mirrors how many of us imagine we did our PhD. It also reflects the way many political scientists work throughout their research careers. But, one of the most obvious ways that interpretivists might make their otherwise idiographic work comparative is to combine it with one or more scholars who have done something similar but in a different setting. Indeed, each of us have found collaboration a fruitful way of managing the depth-breadth trade-off.

Naturalist social scientists increasingly conduct their research in teams or clusters. Rapid international professionalisation, and faster still technological development, make it possible for geographically spread out teams to collate new datasets for comparative analysis. Modelled on the natural science laboratory, this approach depends on using standard protocols to produce uniform and reliable data. Yet the obvious and well-documented perils and pitfalls of the field make this task daunting – and it confronts considerable scepticism from the humanist tradition.

The longest standing alternative remains the 'lone wolf' researcher in the field. Again, this image is tied intimately to the humanist pursuit of idiographic knowledge. As we have already stressed, this stance embraces the uncertainties and unexpectedness of the field, and treats them as a deeply personal, idiosyncratic voyage. It appears anathema to the notion of teamwork.

Producing an explicitly comparative form of interpretive research, however, often requires embracing the prospect of collaboration. To be sure, it cannot be step-by-step, calibrated teamwork in the style of large-scale naturalist field projects. A commitment to humanist endeavour means emphasising the importance of subjective experience to reflexively capture the messiness of the field. It entails eclectic collaboration, and it expands the prospects of drawing comparative and theoretically powerful insights from across studies (e.g. Boswell and Corbett 2017).

At the crux of any such comparison is family resemblances among the dilemmas actors face. In our experience, it is common, when making sense of fieldwork data and opening emerging interpretation to scrutiny, to discover surprising or unforeseen affinities in the work of friends or colleagues. We can point to many examples of our own work where we have teamed with collaborators to combine fieldwork data about different countries, or regions. We learn that monarchs in different contexts face similar dilemmas in democratic transitions (Corbett et al. 2017). We discover that EU officials and NHS managers face similar dilemmas about appearing open and engaging (Iusmen and Boswell 2017). We find that civil society actors in different countries confronting different issues nonetheless face similar dilemmas in trying to influence elite debate (Boswell et al. 2016). These family resemblances only dawn on us afterwards, enabled by a shared commitment to puzzling.

But there is, we suggest, just as much potential in seeking to combine fieldwork insights across substantive and methodological divides. Key here is that just as some common dilemmas emerge unexpectedly, others can be predicted in advance based on shared or overlapping traditions. The latter are the 'family resemblances' that guide a naturalist version of comparison (see Goertz 2006). Take, for example, the Westminster systems discussed in the previous chapter. Regardless of research tradition, fieldwork would provide ample data that could speak to the shared dilemmas experienced by actors across these governments. By basing analysis around common dilemmas across a broad family of cases, this approach has the potential to combine naturalist and humanist research.

Again, Corbett is a good example of this seemingly heretical form of collaboration. The most obvious link between his Pacific cases and the rest of the discipline is to present them as 'small states' and to collaborate with other small state scholars working on different parts of the world. When he teamed up with Wouter Veenendaal, they had to reconcile their epistemological traditions. They considered several possible ways of resolving the tension between their respective approaches. For example, they considered reporting data differently depending on the approach used. This solution follows Furlong and Marsh's (2002) dictum that ontological and epistemological preferences are 'a skin not a sweater'. So, researchers should not compromise their beliefs irrespective of the substantive gains that could be made by taking a more eclectic approach. This quasi-religious stance sits uncomfortably with us. Rather than hem researchers in, the comparative intuition should allow us to break out of the straightjacket-like rules of naturalist social science. Again, we are not claiming that anything goes but rather that one of the advantages that interpretive scholars have is that they possess an intellectual poaching licence to beg, borrow and steal from other ways of doing social science, blurring genres and disciplinary boundaries in the process (see Rhodes 2017). When asked, most political scientists are similarly pragmatic. Kapiszewski, Maclean and Read (2015: 77) found that eclecticism is ubiquitous in US political science. We see no reason for it to be different in other parts of the world. Most researchers are happy melding traditions when doing their own research, and we hope that the comparative intuition we champion will encourage even the staunchest methodological purist to consider collaborating with 'the other side'.

Rule #7: Learn How to Muddle Through

We have described fieldwork as an adventure – even fun – but any adventure has its risks and fieldwork typically has many ups and downs. As Wood (2007: 141) comments 'inadequate attention' is paid to the 'emotional dynamics' of field work. The naturalist may strive to be the detached observer, but the researcher's role varies, at times with bewildering speed – one day a professional stranger (Agar 1996) walking the tightrope between insider and outsider, the next a complete bystander, left behind in the office to twiddle your thumbs, wondering how long exclusion will last. Comparative interpretive fieldwork involves endlessly balancing involvement and detachment. It is a strain, and mistakes are normal, inadvertently changing people's behaviour. The interpretive approach to fieldwork does not consider such changes mistakes. Rather, they are inevitable because the knower and the known are inseparable, interacting and influencing one another, leading to shared interpretations (Lincoln and Guba 1985).

No matter the degree of involvement, all fieldworkers face the challenge of coping. Living away from family and home can lead to attacks of the blues. Like the rock star on the road, one can bewail another night in another cheap hotel. During 'shadowing', actors can refuse to cooperate and withdraw support at any point. 'Snowballing' from interviewee to interviewee means there can be no definitive list, and this can lead to endless worry about access. 'Going where you are led' generates uncertainty about the relevance of the work and, indeed, the aims of the project.

Now add in international travel and residence. There is no comfort zone in comparative interpretive research. The researcher is rarely familiar with the surrounds. They have to deal with upheaval, uncertainty, anxiety, and sometimes challenging climates, inhospitable hotels, ravenous insects and a stomach that rejects the local food and water, often at speed. Travelling brings its own special qualities to the table. Tempers will be tested by queuing at airports, security and customs' checks, taxis that overcharge and airport buses that stop at every hotel but yours.

The serious consequence of these anxieties and discomforts is doubt about the feasibility of the project and the capacities of the researcher. Doubt can lead to ill-advised changes in research design; the sharing of fieldwork stories that breach confidentiality; and inappropriately close relationships with practitioners. Emotional stresses and strains are unavoidable in comparative fieldwork. The real question is how best to cope with, even avoid these pitfalls. Some of our rules of thumb might be helpful in this regard. The notebook can be a source of solace; a place to let off steam. It can be used as a diary of the fieldworker's personal impressions and feelings. For example, in his PhD research, Boswell's notebooks quickly took on a symbolic rather than practical utility. He had been a hopeless note-taker even since his days in undergraduate lectures. He has abysmal handwriting that even he cannot make out later. He kept losing track of which book he was writing in. He sometimes forgot to bring one at all and had to duck into a nearby stationery shop or simply scrawl notes on the back of random scraps of A4. But he still found notebooks useful. On meeting interview participants, for instance – many of whom came from hard science backgrounds – reaching for an old-fashioned notebook clearly signalled to them that this was a more humanistic endeavour, encouraging the relaxed rapport that he sought. It also gave him something to do – or at least to appear to do – as he waited for them or if an interview was interrupted momentarily, to alleviate the social anxieties that such situations can sometimes present. Perhaps more importantly, the evening ritual of writing down observations and impressions, drawing out similarities and differences across contexts, and jotting down new questions or thoughts helped him to make sense of, and feel more in control of, the inevitable confusion and complexity.

Other forms of writing can also be cathartic. For early career researchers standing back to understand what is happening and why can help build confidence. Yo-yoing makes it easier to manage anxieties and emotions because the researcher can regularly engage with colleagues at the university and with family. Collaborative working also helps because troubles can be shared with co-workers. But the lone wolf must still plan to deal with their emotions out in the field.

We accept that there is no one way of coping that will suit everyone – that learning how to muddle through is part of the challenge. There are doubtless many other practical ways to manage the emotional strain. Whatever the preferred means at the core of all such strategies is a reflexive awareness of both self and the challenges of the work.

Conclusion

The many texts on fieldwork practice rarely talk at length about the challenges and pitfalls of doing explicitly comparative work. Instead, the assumption is that we can replicate what works for one field site in a second site. As we have shown, this is only partly true. Indeed, we posit that thinking about comparative fieldwork differently can be incredibly helpful. Our aim, therefore, has been to provide a set of practical 'rules of thumb' that will assist researchers in thinking consciously about their *comparative* fieldwork. As will have become clear from our discussion, each is essentially mutually reinforcing. When we were pragmatic in how we sequenced our project, we were much more likely to start writing sooner. Likewise, when we were open to eclectic collaboration, then we were likely interested in telling stories that resonated with numerous audiences. The key point, therefore, is that while our approach to fieldwork can be used as a step-by-step guide of sorts, it is more accurately conceived of as an orientation towards fieldwork practice. To that end, we have not focused heavily on data collection techniques but on the choices (even dilemmas) that comparison presents to researchers.

The reason this orientation is so important is that, in our experience, it sets the researcher on a path to moving *through* their data. When coupled with the emphasis on finding and interrogating dilemmas (see Chapter 3), this orientation gives the researcher a fighting chance of seeing the theoretical wood from the empirical trees, demystifying creative intuition in the process. In this important sense, analysis and fieldwork are intimately intertwined, explaining in part why writing-up is the second rule of thumb. However, analysis also presents unique challenges of its own, which we address in more detail in the next chapter.

6   Analysis

DISCUSSANT: We all sometimes write papers that rely on retrospectively re-analysing data rather than following a standard research design, so I have sympathy with what you are trying to do. I mean, you have put a lot of work into collecting all of this data so you understandably want to get as much out of it as possible. But it feels a bit to me like you have just taken the most interesting bits of data and used them to create stylised categories that allow you to speak to different theoretical debates than you originally intended.

AUTHOR: Yeah, of course. Why would that be a problem?

DISCUSSANT: Well, it's not very social scientific.

We paraphrase but all three of us has had a version of this exchange with discussants at conferences and workshops, and later with peer reviewers, on more occasions than we care to remember. What we find fascinating is that the criticism can emanate from either side of the naturalist/humanist divide. For naturalists, the long-standing concern is that by retrofitting our research design to accentuate interesting findings we are biasing our analysis. A more recent preoccupation is that we might be misrepresenting or falsifying our data. Discussion in this tradition has culminated recently in support of a new set of standardised protocols on Data Access and Research Transparency (DA-RT) (see Elman and Kapiszewski 2014). The aim of DA-RT is to promote openness and transparency in the ways political scientists report the evidence supporting their research findings. For the types of fieldwork outlined in the previous chapter, it would involve providing reviewers and readers with transcripts, notebooks and coding schemas so they can independently assess the credibility of knowledge claims. Numerous prestigious journals in the field have since adopted DA-RT protocols.

For humanists of a more idiographic persuasion, the concern is that our account is stylised and our categories imposed by the literature rather than emerging organically from the field. Colleagues working in this tradition want to know more about the processes of dwelling with our data that enabled us to 'somehow capture' the multifaceted complexity of social phenomena (Schwartz-Shea and Yanow 2016). These scholars are also more likely to repudiate DA-RT-style protocols on the basis that they are unethical because they threaten the anonymity of respondents and undermine good practice by treating transparency as a substitute for reflexivity (see Schwartz-Shea and Yanow 2016).

In this chapter, we argue that this new focus on how to analyse qualitative data in practice is welcome. In fact, we suggest that we find aspects of both naturalist and humanist discussions productive and constructive. The naturalist account of rigour provides useful tools for undertaking the painstaking evaluation of rival accounts necessary for robust comparative interpretive research. The humanist account of rigour provides useful tools for making holistic sense of messy phenomena in a comparative context. Yet both, we suggest, set the bar rather too high, particularly given the constraints and challenges posed by the greater complexities of comparative research. On the one hand, naturalist procedures are inevitably too rigid for the task at hand. They cannot be sensibly applied across contexts that entail their own complex specificity. On the other hand, those same complexities evade 'capture' in the 'Eureka!' moment envisaged by humanists. There are always loose ends, exceptions, bits of the puzzle that do not fit. Analysis inevitably involves some degree of stylisation and simplification, and these shortcuts and choices are starker in a comparative project.

To forge a way between these two ways of analysing data in this chapter we argue for a consciously *impressionistic* approach to data analysis in comparative interpretive research. We use this term provocatively but also deliberately and carefully – as a shorthand analogy to impressionistic art and not in its pejorative, everyday sense of being haphazard, rushed or shoddy. Adopting an impressionistic orientation unlocks the creative potential of comparative interpretive research.

This chapter explains and justifies this orientation to analysis, before underlining what it means in practice for how the analyst conducts this craft. We return in the conclusion to reflect on what following these rules of thumb might mean for disciplinary debates about rigour in pluralist political science.

Impressionistic Analysis

Key figures in the interpretive approach to studying politics and policy have bristled at the mainstream notion that such research is 'impressionistic'. Wagenaar (2011: 251), in his overview of the core features of interpretive policy analysis, confronts this sticky prejudice:

Those who are critical of interpretive approaches generally tend to see them as unsystematic, impressionistic, 'soft' ways of doing scientific research.

Dvora Yanow (2006: 100) is even more emphatic, 'interpretive' does not mean 'impressionistic'. For these and other key pioneers (e.g. Ospina and Dodge 2005), the aim is to actively and deliberately reclaim this form of research and analysis as equally 'systematic' to naturalist social science.

As the term 'reclaim' would suggest, no one uses 'systematic' in the rigid sense typically employed by naturalists – there is room for creativity, spontaneity and iteration. Instead, the key pioneers of this movement see research as systematic in the sense that it involves a methodical progression towards a more coherent and convincing account of the phenomenon under investigation. Wagenaar (2011: 22) explains:

Through a painstaking and systematic process of imaginative induction, we transform our crude earlier interpretations/observations into better, higher-order more enduring interpretations that somehow capture the meaning of what has transpired.

Likewise, Yanow (2006: 102) describes the work of interpretation as an 'interpretive dance' towards a deeper and more fulfilling understanding, offering the following analogy:

The most exacting descriptions of forms of interpretive analysis describe a kind of indwelling with one's data: whether using index cards held in the hand or large sheets of paper tacked to the walls, the process entails reading and rereading again – musing, in an abductive way – until, in the light of prior knowledge of the theoretical literature or the empirical data, or both, something makes sense in a new way. The experience feels like part of a thousand-piece jigsaw puzzle suddenly fitting together. . .

This analogy is instructive. The notion of a jigsaw puzzle hints at the fact that interpretation must inevitably be framed or restricted. It recognises that there is limited space in which to record interpretations and typical constraints about the ways in which this might occur. It acknowledges also that interpretive researchers are working with different sorts of materials (theoretical and empirical), and captures the sense of intellectual creativity involved in trying to link them together.

Be warned, the creative work of interpretation is messy. The 'pieces' of interpretive research do not always fit together neatly as in a jigsaw puzzle. There is no map or picture on the cover of the box. Rather than completing a puzzle, we are continuously puzzling like policymakers searching for a solution (Heclo 2010 [1974]). Sometimes we force pieces together to get a cleaner or more interesting account. Moreover, there is no expected or ideal end result to interpretive research. Its final form is in no way obvious, and it can take multiple, conflicting forms. Finally, and most fundamentally, the jigsaw puzzle analogy overlooks the fact that there are not a thousand pieces, but an infinite number. This statement applies to both the data and the academic literature. There are no self-evident ways to link scholarly ideas and concerns with data.

The limitations of the jigsaw puzzle analogy point us to the limitations of a shared conception among interpretive scholars that the practices of interpretation entail a systematic progression towards a superior analysis (e.g. Schwartz-Shea and Yanow 2012; Wagenaar 2011). We are not trying to show that our analysis is better than naturalistic inquiry. We do not want to be more concerned with criticising the limits of naturalism than delivering the goods for our preferred approach. Our particular ways of making sense do not always deliver the 'Eureka!' moment. The outcomes are often unstable and contestable. In our experience, a more apt descriptor for the work involved is impressionistic, and a more apt analogy is the creation of impressionist art.

We do not suggest here that in their repudiation of the label 'impressionistic' that Yanow, Wagenaar or anyone else uses this term as a referent to the art world. Taken in context, their usage is more in line with the everyday sense of impressionistic – being vague, hastily reached or uninformed. And, although the apparent contrast works well as a rhetorical device, we do not, in picking up on this term, mean to appeal to these connotations. Instead, we reclaim the meaning of impressionism as associated with the revolutionary art movement of the nineteenth century (see Boswell and Corbett 2015a, 2015b, 2015c). The 'impressionists' went against the conventions of the time, which upheld the virtue of creating smooth portraits of idyllic subjects, and tried instead to capture life as they saw it. Rather than focus on the noble or divine, for instance, they took their inspiration from everyday settings – natural and social – and tried to capture the unique 'impression' of being there. They set about their work in a way that was often informed by particular stylistic motifs – to recreate the play of light – which, in turn, were enabled by particular techniques – especially the use of thick, textured, contrasting brush strokes (Clancy 2003). But impressionism was not a conformist school with a method to be formulaically applied according to a set programme. It was a general orientation with a set of tools that the artist could draw upon with innovative virtuosity (Herbert 1988). It was, above all, an *orientation* to how art ought to be produced.

Seen in this way, an impressionistic orientation is ideally suited to the particular challenges of conducting richly detailed comparative analysis. It is a stance that acknowledges that no analysis can do full justice to the complexities of social and political life. But it also encourages us to focus our analytical attention on the most striking features in the field – in comparative interpretive research, the dilemmas (and responses to dilemmas) we encounter are typically the vibrant dynamics that we seek to illuminate. As such, this orientation allows us to borrow across the established toolkits of qualitative analysis in ways that still entail and ensure richness, rigour and plausibility. But it also mitigates against the risks of analysis-by-paralysis that the humanist tradition of ill-defined 'indwelling' in particular can engender. It releases the creative intuition that lies at the heart of our approach.

The rest of this chapter describes the pragmatic rules of thumb that follow from an impressionistic orientation to analysis.

Rules of Thumb for Analysis

The rules of thumb for analysis are listed in Table 6.1.

Table 6.1 Rules of thumb for analysis

1. Analyse in the moment
2. Analyse through writing
3. Analysis is never finished
4. Use tools of the trade as shortcuts (not answers)
5. Embrace the grind
6. Be open to other interpretations
7. Explore contradictions
8. Think analyses, not analysis

Rule #1: Analyse in the Moment

The 'analysis phase' remains the most mysterious and worrying for the newcomer to qualitative research. The long-held mythology is of the researcher returning from a long stint in the field to an Ivory Tower retreat, cocooned from the outside world, to emerge some months or possibly even years later with a beautiful analysis. Of course, recent writing in both naturalist and humanist tradition has lampooned this tradition, and sought to demystify the process. Kapiszewski, Maclean and Read (2015) in particular shed important light on the practical techniques, tools and processes involved in the hard graft of turning raw qualitative data into convincing analysis and interpretation. Even so, this work of analysis – in accordance with the mythical stepwise approach to research projects that even our own chapter order risks reinforcing – is still typically presented as something that occurs after fieldwork is complete. After all, the data analysis phase should logically occur after the data collection phase.

In our experience, that maxim is only partially and occasionally true – of course analysis requires data to analyse but, as we have discussed at length in Chapter 5, data collection in comparative interpretive research (and in fact in most research projects) is a piecemeal and punctuated exercise. We typically yo-yo in and out of different settings, across fieldwork sites and between the field and the desk. So, there is in fact ample opportunity to analyse in the moment.

More important than opportunity and means is motive: analysing in the moment is not just something that can be done, it is something we recommend doing. While yo-yoing across settings is exciting, it can also often feel somewhat chaotic. It means meeting new people and becoming accustomed to new environments. It will also involve experiencing interrupted work and domestic routines. There are stressfully short turnarounds between meetings in unfamiliar places, and painfully long waits in airport lounges. This disruption can be unsettling and difficult. But it is also precisely when many of us are at our most creative – we are, as impressionists, finding inspiration in affinities and contrasts we experience and observe. It would be crazy *not* to channel this creative energy into preliminary forms of analysis.

Take Corbett's study of Pacific Island politicians as an example. As a PhD student, he transcribed and coded his interviews in the field at night with only the dull roar of the air conditioner for company. He began by grouping interview quotes by theme – those that related to how a politician became interested in politics, how they won their first election, how they interpreted corruption, etc. He used the software package NVivo to undertake this task. When collections of quotes became too large – more than twenty or so – he would start to break them down into sub-themes. So, how a politician became interested in politics broke down into sub-themes of those who had a parent in politics, or those who became politically active at university, etc. The patterns that emerged either supported, challenged or nuanced the initial findings from previously analysed autobiographies/biographies. None of these categories were ever 'finalized' – Corbett did interviews right up until the book was published – and for later projects he reanalysed the data to answer new questions. More importantly, by analysing in the moment he was able to manage his comparative fieldwork across 14 countries because he had emerging findings to discuss with interviewees in new contexts. Specifically, he could play the role of informed insider, using questions like 'In country X things work like this, is it the same here?' Inevitably the answer was a version of: 'yes, but with some differences'. By analysing in the moment he was able to channel the energy and enthusiasm that stems from learning new things rather than waiting for a 'Eureka!' moment when everything crystallised.

Rule #2: Analyse through Writing

If the artificial separation between analysis and data collection remains a reassuring myth that social scientists largely adhere to, then the equivalent separation between analysis and writing is one that is beginning to be subjected to scrutiny, at least within the interpretive tradition (see especially Law 2004; van Maanen 1988 and Yanow 2009 for lengthy treatments). We will cover writing in more detail in Chapter 7, but for now the important point is that leading authors in this vein have written at length about the crucial role that writing plays in thinking about data and thinking through the patterns exhibited therein. The argument is that writing-up findings in social science *is* thinking. It is only when attempting to write up fieldwork that emergent themes crystallise. We realise previously held interpretations do not hold; that trends and patterns link together in previously unseen ways; and that new interpretations emerge and take shape to make better sense of the 'mess' encountered in the field. We would argue that such writing-up is even more important for explicitly comparative projects because moving between field sites magnifies the 'mess'.

The focus in this existing work, however, remains squarely on writing itself. The emphasis is on dwelling on what makes writing such a creative, frustrating, non-linear activity. There is little reflection back on what these inconvenient truths about writing mean for the work of analysis. If writing is thinking, then this confounds any sense of analysis as being a systematic and detached process. Our suggestion, in line with the by now familiar philosophy of the book, is not to resist the messiness, but to go with it. The inevitable confusion that arises out of writing-up comparative interpretive research should not lead practitioners to wall off artificially the process of analysis, but to embrace the ways in which writing can feed into and enhance analysis. It is an invitation to analyse *through* writing.

To be clear, we do not have in mind here the sort of writing that occurs in fieldwork notebooks – i.e. the sort of writing that we are *supposed* to do in the field according to established traditions. Naturally, writing in a fieldwork notebook can and does push along the analytical process. We jot ideas, trends, patterns down as well as observations to make sense of what we are experiencing. Indeed, in our experience, the fieldwork notebook exemplifies how the boundaries between analysis and data collection can blur. But this writing is not the sort that exposes gaps, problems and limitations in interpretation. Such gaps only become glaring in academic prose. In the context of comparative interpretive research, we are talking about a taboo in both naturalist and interpretive traditions. We are talking about provisional writing-up *in* the field. Only through this sort of writing is it possible to test and flesh out emergent analytical categories during and in between site visits. Doing so forces us to train our eye on the key dilemmas in the field and trace out the relevant responses in practice. It helps identify gaps, omissions, misconceptions in initial interpretations and guides and shapes future field research.

We can take as an example Boswell's comparative study of obesity politics in Australia and the UK. The field research took place in Australia first, and the immediate and overwhelming impression from this initial research was the universal and near constant appeal by policy actors to 'evidence-based policymaking'. He spent the few months in between field visits trying to work out what this 'fetish' for evidence meant, and presented the first draft of his initial insights at a series of conferences. This early writing-up revealed limitations that prompted subsequent fieldwork in the UK. This work confirmed some initial insights but, more important, significantly augmented and challenged others. The dilemmas evident in the field to various actors about what evidence ought to count, what the evidence means, and how the evidence should be interpreted to influence policymaking were common in both settings. However, the responses of actors across both sites revealed important differences (a bolder form of advocacy in the UK, for instance). The commitment to writing-up initial analytical categories helped to channel the later field research, but did not unduly constrain it or forestall the prospect of surprise. More significantly, Boswell would not have known he needed to do this comparative fieldwork if he had not begun his analysis in the moment.

Rule #3: Analysis Is Never Finished

Our final point about process is that analysis is never complete in any definitive sense. Naturally, there is an inclination to 'move on' from long-running projects, especially once key publications have emerged. But in comparative interpretive research especially, existing datasets can function as vital stores for later analysis. A subsequent project in a new timeframe, region or sector, or one focused on a different set of actors or organisations, might throw up important potential comparisons for future analysis. In fact, in our experience, it is likely to. Indeed, if we take the point made in the previous chapter about embracing collaboration to unlock comparative potential seriously, then any form of data can be reinvented for another purpose. It is only natural to make sense of new and perplexing experiences in the field in relation to previous experiences, to spot unforeseen or unexpected parallels between seemingly different contexts. Particularly crucial here is the fact that new research can shed light on the gaps or cracks in previous work. It can help make sense of the bits of the puzzle that never fitted and that gnaw away in the back of our minds. It is vitally important, then, to be prepared and willing to go back and mine the old dataset and flesh out any potential affinities with new work.

A good example of this is Rhodes' work on government departments, which led to work on both Chiefs of Staff (see Chapter 4) and gender. Rhodes' (2011) original study was not concerned with how gender played out in the workings of the departmental courts, or with the consequences. Mackay and Rhodes (2013) reanalysed the data, but this time using gender identification as a basis for comparison. They asked how the bureaucratic beliefs and practices of the departmental court reproduced gender relations. They asked also, what were the gendered consequences of such everyday practices? Their data show the day-to-day practices of the departmental courts reproduce gendered inequalities. They are 'greedy institutions' (Coser 1974), which leave no space for either family or social life. The protocols and ritualised practices are coping mechanisms through which the departmental court maintains continuity, and through which institutional reform and innovation, including equal opportunity reforms, can be adopted, adapted and resisted. So, the status quo is not challenged. One significant gender consequence is that women have few institutional options but to 'manage like men'.

There were gaps and silences in the data because there were few senior women civil servants or ministers in 2002. In addition, the interviews and fieldwork observations were for citation but not for attribution. With so few women in the study, preserving anonymity made it difficult, for example, to compare male and female career trajectories without it being obvious who respondents were. Indeed, to preserve anonymity in the original study, Rhodes used the masculine pronoun in reporting data on ministers and permanent secretaries unless he had permission to waive anonymity. Nonetheless, this analysis demonstrated that fresh insights can be gained by applying a gender perspective to data gathered for another purpose.

The point of all three of these procedural rules of thumb is that analysis is not a discrete activity that occurs during a settled period of 'desk work'. It is, like all parts of comparative interpretive research, inevitably inflected with and affected by other tasks and priorities. This statement applies to all types of research, but it is particularly important that we acknowledge, rather than down play, these influences in an explicitly comparative project where the potential for moving parts and 'mess' is magnified. In these circumstances, our process orientated rules of thumb are not just a more honest reflection on practice, but a necessary pragmatic strategy for ensuring the project gets done.

Another advantage of treating analysis as an iterative, continuing task intertwined with fieldwork and writing-up is a rarely acknowledged psychological one. It provides the confidence necessary to scale the inevitable 'mountain of data'. The overwhelming question when presented with a rich and deep qualitative dataset that covers multiple field sites is simply where to begin. But getting into the habit of analysing in the moment, and writing-up in academic prose as we go, can make this task seem more manageable. It is here that the impressionism metaphor is apt. We do not take pre-determined pieces and fit them into a puzzle or sketch the outline onto the canvas and then fill in the blank spaces. We paint straight on to the canvas, and then when it dries we paint over it again, and again and again. Each brush stroke brings new light, texture and colour to the picture. Not every addition makes it better. We often re-code quotes, delete sections and even at times start all over again. These are not failures; they are part of any creative process worth doing.

Rule #4: Use Tools of the Trade as Shortcuts (Not Answers)

Even in light of the above discussion, it is important to stress one abiding truth about qualitative research in the social sciences – the proverbial 'mountain of data' is unavoidable. Indeed, it is doubly unavoidable in comparative interpretive work. Field researchers, especially first-timers, are often overwhelmed when returning from the field. They have amassed an immense volume of data, often hundreds of documents, dozens of interview transcripts, pages of field notes. A comparative project can double, triple or quadruple that volume even if the time spent in each field site is less. The recent proliferation of work on qualitative and interpretive analysis has sought to demystify this process and provide researchers with techniques to analyse their data (e.g. Braun and Clarke 2006; Gee 2004; Hajer 2009). Competing visions abound – variations on discourse, narrative and framing analysis, versions of 'practice theory', dramaturgical and rhetorical approaches, thematic analysis and so on. Our basic stance is that these 'tools of the trade' are useful guides, but nothing like the 'recipes' that many students of the craft crave. They serve a valuable role in giving a sense of direction to initial analysis. They imbue confidence and set out a clear structure for how analytical work can proceed. But, after a while, their limitations in the 'mess' of real-world datasets become readily apparent. Distinctive narratives begin to blend at the edges. Discrete themes start to overlap. Worst of all, key insights begin to fall by the wayside, unable to fit neatly into any categorical box. That sense of purpose and confidence ebbs away.

We often use analytical tools such as thematic analysis, performative analysis and discourse analysis. They help us think systematically about an issue, problem or puzzle. They are an intellectual shortcut that can help us better understand the topic at hand. But they also leave room for ambiguity: their meaning and function is always open to revision and reconsideration. They are not right or wrong but a tool for uncovering new ideas. When we use discourse analysis or some other technique, they produce stylised representations. They do not allow us to say everything we would like to say about our data. Instead, they are most useful as a way of simplifying the data, identifying dilemmas and suggesting plausible conjectures.

For example, take Boswell's account of obesity politics in the UK and Australia. This research generated thousands of documents, dozens of interviews, dozens of hours of video footage across both sites. Boswell adopted and adapted the 'recipe' of narrative analysis to cut through the debate, organising it into six competing narratives about obesity policy. This initial analysis helped to outline the key contours and frontiers of public debate, representing an important contribution in its own right. But it was only the essential first step in setting the scene for the analysis at the heart of the project, which was trained on the dilemmas around how advocates of these competing narratives sought to use evidence and expertise; how they negotiated their representative role; and how they navigated different sites of debate. The toolkit associated with narrative analysis served a role in stylising and simplifying the comparative context sufficiently for the higher-level analysis to make sense.

The other point is that established 'techniques' in the social sciences are not the only way forward – we can look further afield, to the humanities and the arts, for other ways to do the same work. Rhodes (2017b; chapter 1) suggests that we blur genres by drawing on analogies and metaphors from the humanities. We should look at politics as 'as a serious game, a sidewalk drama, or a behavioural text' (Geertz 1983: 21). We can look to the humanities for new ideas about both genres of thought (such as hermeneutics, interpretivist) and genres of presentation (see Chapter 7). Such poaching is about 'edification' – a way of finding 'new, better, more interesting, more fruitful ways of speaking about' comparative research (Rorty 1980: 360). For example, Hodgett and Rhodes (in press) explore the ways in which the visual arts contribute to area studies. Their examples include a photographic essay on the capital buildings of the American states. Goodsell (1988, 2001) concludes these buildings are an example of soft power that sustains citizen identification with the regime. His case study is a good example of the comparative analysis of both the contested and consensual meaning of public architecture (see also Yanow 2013).

Rule #5: Embrace the Grind

As well as a proliferation of recipe-style techniques for coping with the 'mountain of data' problem, there is also a growing market in software packages to assist in this task. The appeal of surrendering to the machine in this way is obvious: for researchers of a naturalist persuasion, it lends a sense of objectivity and systematic analysis to a notoriously subjective enterprise (see, for example, Klüver 2009). For researchers of any persuasion, it promises to relieve the heavy grind of working through the dataset manually. In our experience of comparative interpretive research, the first appeal represents a fallacy, and the second wishful thinking. In this section, we deal with the latter first before returning to the former.

First, we stress that in the comparative interpretive search to uncover dilemmas and the beliefs and traditions in which they are situated, no software package can replace the value of dwelling with the data. Simply put, uncovering dilemmas requires the sort of deep contextual interpretation that only comes from the grind of reading, thinking, rereading and rethinking iteratively. If the 'recipes' discussed in the prior section imbue a useful initial sense of purpose and confidence, the risk with software programmes is an abiding overconfidence. The high-tech trappings and the technical language can disguise the reality that 'coding' in this manner is, for most users, simply the process of identifying and highlighting key words and phrases and having them copied and pasted into new files. The risk in having too much faith in the machine is that data become de-contextualised – unpacking the complexities of context specificity remains the trump card of qualitative research.

However, we do acknowledge that software programmes can play important analytical roles within this paradigm. They can usefully highlight excerpts for attention within an impossibly large dataset. They can graphically illustrate overwhelming patterns in the data for rhetorical effect, using tools like word frequency counts, idea clouds and so on. Perhaps principally, they can function as accessible and up-to-date repositories for manual coding – something particularly useful when travelling frequently, or working in teams. But in each case, the software is merely any accoutrement to dwelling with the data. There is no substitute for grind.

Second, we push back against the impression that computer-assisted coding is superior because of its supposedly objective nature. As explained at length in Chapter 2, embracing interpretive research requires embracing a subjective orientation anyway. Besides these philosophical commitments, there are also key pragmatic benefits in the practice of analysis in comparative interpretive research. Simply put, supposedly 'objective' coding might be a poor way to identify and tease out intriguing comparisons in the unorthodox fashion we promote. Anyone surrendering to the machine will likely struggle to identify parallels in the dilemmas of the French president and the leader of an Indian village, or indeed Tony and Edna. But we suggest this problem may also afflict analysts who remain committed to indwelling with their data and are merely using programmes like NVivo to store and organise their analysis. Analysis in comparative interpretive research is, above all, a *creative* enterprise. Manual coding in its most rudimentary form – done with old-fashioned paper, coloured pens, highlighters, folders, post-it notes and index cards – is a tactile process that lends itself (at least for many people) to the sort of creativity involved in augmenting, tweaking and challenging emergent analytical categories. The computer can aid this process but it cannot replace it.

Take Corbett's (2015a) book on politicians, for example. Corbett's data included more than 100 interviews and more than fifty autobiographies/biographies, combined with numerous published interviews and secondary material. He used NVivo to code this material thematically. The advantage of NVivo was that it enabled him to move quotes from theme to theme while retaining the integrity of the initial transcript or data source. It was also easier for him to place the same quote in multiple codes because each phrase could have multiple uses. At the same time, simple word searches and other similar tools would have struggled to produce meaningful results for interviews conducted across 14 countries, combined with books authored over four decades, and sources compiled by other authors. Corbett had to work with each data source. He had to account for the context of each quote when employing it in his analysis. Moreover, to provide a truly decentred account, who was speaking mattered as much as what was said. Tribal allegiances, for example, are a recurring motif in the literature on Pacific politics, to the extent that many authors claim they are deterministic. To decentre, Corbett had to push back against this argument while also acknowledging that it shaped the way many actors saw their role. So, when talking about tribes, he used quotes by Indo-Fijian politicians (e.g. Corbett 2015a: 42), who are said to have no tribes, to illustrate how such practices and rhetorical appeals influenced the practice of politics. He made the same move to refute claims about ethnic differences between regions of the Pacific. He used quotes about ascribed leadership by Melanesians, whose leadership style is famously gained rather than given (e.g. Corbett 2015a: 28) or electoral system (e.g. Corbett 2015a: 68). Such nuances, undetected by most readers but essential to the integrity of the overall argument, could not have been made without substantial dwelling with the data, because the most sophisticated computer program will struggle to capture such subtleties.

Rule #6: Be Open to Other Interpretations

Our emphasis on deep indwelling might appear to reinforce the long-held tradition of qualitative analysis as a lone and aloof pursuit. We do not wish to give this impression. Like most creative processes, the work of analysis benefits from the spark of discussion, criticism and contention that comes from social interaction. It can be enormously valuable to 'open up' the practice of analysis, particularly with research participants who have deep contextual understanding. But opening up does not mean surrendering control. In comparative interpretive research especially, the trick is in finding the right balance.

In this discussion, we take particular inspiration from the recent flowering of work within the interpretive tradition on the value of opening up the practice of analysis (see especially Braa, Monteiro and Sahay 2004; Orr and Bennett 2009; Ospina and Dodge 2005; Wagenaar 2012). We agree with these authors that there are significant benefits to be gained from involving research participants in the analysis of data. In fact, in the context of comparative research where the analyst has to show mastery of multiple case contexts, these benefits are even more apparent. Participants can provide vital insights into contextual misperceptions, errors and omissions that make the overall analysis more accurate and robust.

Yet there is the risk that participants will steer interpretations too strongly. In particular, there is a tendency for participants to see their own situation as unique and special, and to resist efforts to draw comparisons in experience, especially with unorthodox or unlikely contexts. Such feedback can be valuable, of course, but it can also reveal an idiographic parochialism that, if taken too seriously, might blunt the insights comparative interpretive research has to offer. Conceptually, we return to the discussion of how to navigate this terrain in greater depth in the conclusions (Chapter 8), where we reflect on the ethics of comparative interpretive research. Here, however, we seek to demonstrate the point with the example of Boswell et al.'s (2019) recent comparative study of newly emergent public health bodies in Australia, New Zealand and England.

Boswell and his co-authors presented preliminary insights to a few interested participants. Some were insistent that the particularities of the cases – differences in political histories, institutional arrangements and policy remits – made comparison fraught. Others, however, saw great value in their attempts to compare these bodies. Indeed, they encouraged the researchers to look further afield, to the experience of Thailand, to encompass a greater diversity of experiences and contexts. In the end, the research team sided with the optimists and may well seek to expand the comparative project in the way these readers envisage. The broader point is that comparative analysis might mean drawing affinities that not all of the participants intimately involved in our cases have interest in or awareness of.

Rule #7: Explore Contradictions

Naturalists seek to demonstrate that they have the story 'right', using tri-angulation and other tests to demonstrate the validity of the inferences they have drawn. We take no issue with the careful and painstaking practices associated with triangulation. We agree it is a hallmark of good qualitative research practice and an integral way of maintaining standards. Therefore, we draw on three sources of information:

. . . the pattern of practice, talk, and considered writing – the first is the most reliable, the second is the most copious and revealing and the third is the most difficult to interpret. (Oakeshott 1996: x)

In particular, we look behind the data and compare what people say they do in interviews, and what they do when we observe them in their everyday lives.

The problem is that our various sources of data can and do conflict. All interpretive projects confront this issue, but it is more acute for comparative projects with more moving parts. The first step is to ask people to explain the contradiction. Sometimes the explanation is obvious. For example, Rhodes (2011: chapter 9) was struck by the endless crises confronting government departments. While he was shadowing ministers and permanent secretaries, every department had a crisis. For example, the environment department had foot-and-mouth disease, and the industry department had the collapse of British Energy. In interviews, top civil servants resisted any suggestion that they regularly confronted crises and insisted they coped 'because one is able to control and shape the timetable and the decision-making processes'. They preferred to dismiss their regular crises as 'a one-off'. Everyone told Rhodes about recent crises. Everyone told him it was exceptional – 'it's not like this normally'. Maybe, but compared to universities, or local government – two other types of organisations with which Rhodes was familiar – life in a government department was more demanding because it existed in a media goldfish bowl that can take any problem and make it a crisis. Rhodes resolved this contradiction by distinguishing between situational crises, which are threatening and urgent events out there, and institutional crises, which are revelations about their own shortcomings (following Boin et al. 2005: 139). They may struggle to cope with the rude surprises out there, but with routine crises they cope using their existing repertoire of tools. For top public servants, it is important not to create a crisis by so labelling an event. Whether an event becomes a crisis depends on whether the actors define it as such. A crisis is in the eyes of the several beholders. The contradiction between observation and interviews was resolved.

It is not always so straightforward. People will deny there is any contradiction and try to argue it away. Sometimes, reasonably, we received a Gallic shrug, and the explanation that life is messy, not ordered; 'that's what it's like in the real world'. Sometimes it just does not matter. All researchers can do, must do, is exercise their judgement and make it clear to the reader that is what they are doing, and why. Triangulation is an aid to rigorous analysis, not a panacea for the complexity that is fieldwork.

Rule #8: Think Analyses, Not Analysis

Our final rule of thumb concerns the inevitable worry that we will never conquer the 'mountain of data' and in doing so produce a definitive and infallible analysis. The truth, we are sorry to say, is that we have never reached the top. Much is written about the painstakingly iterative, often entirely circuitous path of interpretive analysis but little is devoted to this final question – have I got the analysis right? (cf. Corbett 2014; t'Hart 2007). The abiding impression is that the researcher reaches, after sufficient immersion, a glorious epiphany that 'somehow captures' the complex dynamics under study. In our experience, it does not work that way. There are minor epiphanies along the way – the products of creative flashes that make the process exciting and worthwhile – but, as we stressed earlier, we have never experienced a sense of having captured 'everything'. There are always loose ends, bits of the puzzle that do not fit in the analytical categories eventually settled on. In comparative interpretive research, these doubts are only amplified. There are many more loose ends, many more leftover puzzle pieces.

The secret here is to think of analysis not as a singular task of capturing everything. Instead, any large dataset warrants multiple analyses that individually capture something of interest, and collectively work towards better capturing everything. The comparative interpretive emphasis on dilemmas is key to understanding and developing this approach in practice.

In any dataset, the analyst is likely to encounter different sorts of dilemmas, or to put it another way, dilemmas that are interesting to different sorts of academic audiences. Indeed, as discussed in the previous chapter on fieldwork, this is the main strength of analysis in this tradition; the material can be put to many uses and answer many questions. Dilemmas that are insignificant, or unremarkable, to one audience can be path breaking in another. Current events given new meaning to old practices. The task, literally, never ends.

Let us take Boswell's comparative study of obesity politics as an example again. One set of dilemmas, which attracted him to the field in the first place, were those confronting government actors in their capacity to steer debate and channel policy action. The issues were whether to take radical action in advance of sound evidence or whether to wait until the problem escalated; how to reconcile the views of powerful corporate interests and respected experts; and how to maintain legitimacy for the governance process despite disappointing many of the actors involved. These dilemmas speak to clear topics of interest in the field of democratic governance, around evidence-based policymaking, networked governance and collaboration. But another set of dilemmas that emerged were those confronting public health advocates trying to influence change: whether to risk scientific credibility in pursuit of policy impact; whether to stay 'inside the tent' and participate in governance processes or 'chuck rocks' from the outside; and ultimately how to ration and channel advocacy efforts in a 'losing battle'. These dilemmas speak to emerging concerns in the public health literature, around the 'impact agenda' in public health and the politicisation of public health expertise. It was not possible, in a single coherent analysis for a single coherent manuscript, to do justice to all of these emergent themes. However, it was possible to conduct multiple analyses (or at least multiple variants of the analysis) for multiple outputs. It would still be hubris to suggest this approach 'somehow captures' the dynamics at play, but it has generated a broader body of work that has been able to tease out these different sets of dilemmas in fuller colour (see Boswell 2014, 2015, 2016a, 2016b; Boswell and Corbett 2015d).

Conclusion

Analysing data is not alchemy – we can and should be more open about how we approach the processes and practices of this core academic skill. There are two main traditions to which qualitative researchers adhere when analysing data. One is the naturalist tradition that seeks to approximate or mimic as many of the procedures favoured by quantitative researchers. This tradition is responsible for the new DA-RT initiative and its emphasis on research transparency. The main alternative is the humanist tradition which seeks to promote greater reflexivity about processes of dwelling with one's data that enables the analyst to 'somehow capture' the multifaceted complexity of complex social phenomena.

Both traditions have their advantages. The naturalist account of rigour gives us useful tools for undertaking the triangulation of rival accounts necessary for robust comparative interpretive research. The humanist account of rigour gives us useful tools for making holistic sense of messy phenomena in a comparative context. The problem, as our brief anecdote at the beginning of the chapter highlights, is that both set the bar rather too high, especially for explicitly comparative research. Naturalist procedures are inevitably too rigid for capturing complex specificity across multiple contexts. Similarly, those same complexities evade 'capture' in the 'Eureka!' moment envisaged by some humanists.

Our approach is in sympathy with the humanist focus on reflexivity, but embraces, rather than suppresses, an impressionistic style. It asks the researcher to celebrate the fact that there are always loose ends, exceptions, bits of the puzzle that do not fit. It recognises that analysis inevitably involves some degree of stylisation and simplification, and these shortcuts and choices are starker in a comparative project. The goal, as we will discuss in the next chapter, is not transparency or stepwise progression – although intellectual honesty about data collection is important – but rather to allow the reader to see the brushstrokes by letting others, be they researchers or participants, observe and judge our work. So, we have to render an account that is intuitively recognisable to the casual observer while retaining enough grist and nuance for the substantive expert. It blends data collection, analysis and writing together 'in the moment'. Thus far, we have provided rules of thumb for data collection and analysis. Both have emphasised that we should start writing 'straight away'. In the next chapter, we focus on how to do so.

7 The Craft of Writing

While co-authoring this book, Boswell was also involved in a project investigating the lived experience of deprivation on the affluent South Coast of England (Boswell et al. 2018). Attentive readers may recall Edna's story from Chapter 3. The fieldwork compared the experience of deprivation in eight neighbourhoods spread across the region. The objective was to determine how people experience deprivation in a context of relative affluence compared to a context of widespread deprivation. The initial design – pairing four deprived neighbourhoods with four affluent neighbourhoods – was a classic 'most different' design common to mainstream comparative research. In practice, though, experience in the field tilted the inquiry off this neat axis. The team found some discrepancies according to relative affluence (as expected), but more according to geographical context (less expected). More important still, they noted far more similarities than differences across all the fieldwork sites (not expected). They painstakingly developed a coding scheme to tease these nuanced findings apart. From here, writing-up should have been a straightforward exercise in committing these codes to paper, right? No such luck.

Anyone familiar with writing-up research in any form will recognise that 'straightforward' is a naïve expectation. Analysis, no matter how thoroughly coded, does not write itself. The team still faced stark dilemmas. Should they structure their written account according to the initial design, or abandon that in favour of a thematic account derived inductively from the data? Should they present the findings with an air of detached authority, or engage in more evocative devices? Should they focus on the detail of specific cases, or foreground their contribution to broader academic and policy debates? In the end, with differing inclinations across the team and with deadlines looming into view, they stumbled to a messy compromise. They continue to muddle through in their efforts to tell their stories to interested audiences.

Boswell's experience reflects the broader challenges of designing, conducting and analysing comparative fieldwork that come to a head in the process of writing-up. The purpose of this chapter is to be open about practices of writing, and to reflect on strategies for communicating comparative interpretive research. We offer no fixed rules, only rules of thumb to be followed more or less closely depending on the project at hand.

We want to clarify at the outset that much of what we have to say about writing is not unique to comparative interpretive research. In fact, we expect that aspects of our discussion will resonate with social scientists of *any* persuasion. Writing-up social science research is never straightforward, whatever the genre. Writing is, above all, a craft – an oftentimes challenging, frustrating and exhausting one, compensated by the fact it can equally be creative, energising and satisfying. We can all learn from reflecting on the experiences and strategies of others engaged in the craft.

Much of what we say will be familiar to humanists working in the idiographic tradition. A commitment to an interpretive orientation entails a commitment to experimentation and iteration in writing. There is no generic formula to help structure the account. To be sure, seeking to compare can multiply and compound this sense of indeterminacy. But, in our experience, many of the challenges (and opportunities) associated with creative freedom are of the same fundamental kind.

Writing comparative interpretive research is a ride on a rapid and rollicking rollercoaster. The ride revolves around the question of who we are trying to talk to. In writing-up, the audience, long lingering in the background, begins to loom large. We think more about how our research might be received, who might want to read it and how we might best communicate our findings to these audiences. Comparative interpretive research has multiple audiences. The aim is to speak *both* to specialist interpretivists *and* general comparativists interested in the broader theoretical implications. We have already argued that a diverse readership is a good thing. We all spend a lot of time on our research, so most of us want as many people as possible to read what we have to say. But speaking across audiences is not without its challenges, as anyone who has attempted to cross disciplinary lines before will know (e.g. Greaves and Grant 2010). In comparative interpretive research, audiences often have different expectations and assumptions. The hard part is working out how to communicate with as many readers as possible while ensuring both clarity of argument and integrity of the empirical research. So, we offer a set of rules of thumb which can help those seeking to respond to and meet those challenges. We start with the fundamental dilemmas in comparative interpretive writing.

The Dilemmas of Writing-Up Comparative Interpretive Research

When writing-up comparative interpretive research, we often confront a feeling of being stuck between – and of violating the norms of – the two main traditions of academic prose in social and political research. The philosophical commitment to an interpretive approach lends itself to particular ways of writing-up, which can be alien or confronting to naturalist readers. But interpretivist norms of writing also have to conform to the diversity, breadth and complexity of a comparative project. We focus on three dilemmas: structure, style and substance. We present each trade-off as a binary: contextual versus thematic; linear versus evocative; breadth versus depth. We know it is a little more complex than these dichotomies suggest. Nevertheless, we see value in this initial stylised presentation as a rhetorical device to prompt thought and reflection on how we imagine audiences, and how we might seek to communicate with them. Some readers may take umbrage with it. But we persist because we think it is precisely the sort of device required to communicate comparative interpretive research effectively.

The Dilemma of Structure: Contextual versus Thematic

The first and most confronting dilemma is about structuring the comparison. How should the material be organised so that it best speaks to different audiences? The main choice is between a contextual and a thematic approach.

A contextual account is one that dwells on the different contexts under examination. Here, the author tackles each case in sequential order. In a thesis or book, the cases become discrete chapters. In an article, they become sections. Unfolding the story in this way is intuitive, and fits with the norms of both naturalist and humanist scholarship. But it can also be severely limiting in comparative interpretive research. Foregrounding context can serve to downplay or obscure broader patterns or affinities across the cases that may be of greatest interest.

The main alternative is a thematic account. Here, the writing is organised in recurring themes across the field research, with the nuances of different cases coming and going across the broader narrative. What constitutes a theme in this sense is open to wide variety and experimentation – the text might be organised around, for instance, common dilemmas that recur for actors regardless of context (see Corbett 2015a) or competing narratives that resonate across field sites (see Boswell 2016a). More imaginative minds than ours have used creative rhetorical devices that enable the story to be told in interesting ways. For example, Pachirat's (2011) evocative account of the social and political implications of animal slaughter, *Every Twelve Seconds*, is organised by the perspectives of the actors – the narrative turns around the differing points of view of key actors engaged in the process. Or, to use an explicitly comparative example, Schaffer's (2008) *The Hidden Costs of Clean Election Reform* is structured around four groups of actors – lawmakers, election officials, party organisers and civic educators. This approach allows him to identify patterns and lessons in case material drawn from all over the world. Regardless of how the text is organised, the chief advantage of a thematic account is that it enables the researcher to headline their broader theoretical contribution. It can also – at least in our experience – be more creative, exciting and fun to produce. But a thematic account is also often harder to explain and justify to reviewers. For qualitative researchers in the naturalist tradition, it violates the standard formula. Their response is often to question whether a comparison is sufficiently rigorous or systematic. For those in the idiographic tradition, this form of writing-up plays into suspicions that comparison flattens context and misses nuance.

The Dilemma of Style: Evocative versus Linear

The second dilemma is about what style to adopt. How do we develop an 'authentic voice' which speaks to diverse audiences?

We have spent a great deal of time and energy in this book extolling the virtues of comparative interpretive research in tapping into and embracing creativity (in the Big-C sense of the term). Writing-up comparative interpretive research can be a culmination or expression of this creativity. The skills of writing-up fieldwork can blur into the skills of writing in other genres because we seek to *evoke* the everyday life and its dilemmas of others. There can be significant scope to experiment with form, for example, when writing a book. Evocative writing is the sort of scholarship we – and most other scholars of a humanist persuasion – find interesting, exciting, inspiring.

However, a dose of pragmatism may well be in order. Not all audiences are so open to artistic flourishes. In some fields, there is a limit to how far the template can be stretched, irrespective of seniority. Linear writing is the order of the day. Linear writing follows a formula modelled on hypothesis testing in hard science academic articles. Linear writing suggests we follow a plan in which topic follows topic in an orderly sequence. It is, to be clear, a narrative device. Research never proceeds in this way, and the writing-up is seldom as seamless as it might seem (see Wildavsky 2010: 10–12). But the way the story is eventually told is neat, logical, orderly and efficient. Though anathema to the humanist orientation, there may arise a need to hold our nose and embrace the more prosaic form of Pro-C creativity. Telling a linear account can be important if we want our insights to be taken seriously and read by certain audiences.

The Dilemma of Substance: Depth versus Breadth

Questions of structure and style in how we try to write for different audiences are of crucial importance. But the enduring challenge for comparative interpretive research surrounds the question of substance – we have limited words to work with, and limited time and attention to capture from readers, so what should we spend most of our time talking about? The issue is that different audiences are reading for and focusing on different things. To appease those in the humanist tradition, the task is to demonstrate deep and nuanced understanding of the case – to display a strong enough command of the material to convince area or context specialists across *multiple* areas or contexts that our research conforms to traditional standards of qualitative rigour. To appease those in the naturalist tradition, on the other hand, the task is to demonstrate theoretical parsimony – to identify conjectures that can plausibly travel to the broader class or category of case in which other social scientists are interested.

The particular Catch 22 is around publication strategy. We can feel caught between the need to conform to the standards of rigour in interpretive research by demonstrating deep and nuanced understanding of the case, and the need to get published in academic journals with a standard word limit of around 8,000 words. To be sure, this is a problem for all qualitative researchers, but it is especially significant for comparative researchers as they must be able to convey the depth of understanding typical of a single case within the same word limit. One way around this problem is to write books instead of articles. But, while a more generous word count is helpful, it ameliorates rather than resolves the dilemma about which style of

Table 7.1 Rules of thumb for the craft of writing

The dilemma of structure
1. Don't wait for the muse to arrive
2. Use writing as a form of thinking
3. Stylise your findings

The dilemma of style
4. Be both linear and evocative
5. Experiment with form and genre
6. Be flexible in how you talk about your work
7. Practice the art of translation

The dilemma of substance
8. Hustle and recycle
9. Share your work early and widely
10. Seek input from the field

writing-up will best suit the material. Also, it ignores the pragmatic imperative for PhDs and Early Career Researchers who need to demonstrate they can write both articles and books. Indeed, in the UK job market, the ability to write both articles and books is essential for any qualitative researcher. Annual performance appraisals expect and reward a consistent ticking over of journal articles, whereas external assessment views monographs as the gold standard. In writing, the perennial breadth versus depth trade-off – something which influences every step of a comparative interpretive project – comes to a head.

Overall, our stance is that these three dilemmas cannot be 'resolved'. In Table 7.1, we offer some rules of thumb for trying to cope with them, and to ensure these dilemmas do not engender a sense of paralysis at the sight of the blank page. As ever, we do not claim they offer a magic recipe. To repeat, we expect everyone – whether interpretivist or naturalist, comparative or idiographic – will recognise and see some value in at least some of them. Likewise, they may not all apply to, or be useful for, all comparative interpretive projects. But we hope they can inform and prompt further reflection for the challenges ahead.

Addressing the Dilemma of Structure

The most intractable of problems in presenting fieldwork is how to turn 'such unruly experience … into an authoritative written account' (van Maanen 1988: 2; see also Clifford 1988; Clifford and Marcus 1986; Geertz

1988: chapter 6; Hammersley 1990)? Van Maanen's (1988: 35) 'war whoop' of an answer is to declare 'there is no way of seeing, hearing, or representing the world of others that is absolutely, universally valid or correct'. He uses the term 'tale', 'quite self-consciously to highlight the presentational or, more properly, representational qualities of fieldwork writing' (van Maanen 1988: 8 and 14). The emphasis falls on writing-up fieldwork that has an 'inherently story-like character', and authors have 'inevitable choices' to make about how they will present their findings (van Maanen 1988).

In comparative interpretive research, it can be an especially daunting challenge. There is no formula or template to follow (as in a naturalist tradition), nor even long-established tropes and traditions to utilise (as in idiographic writing). This can be exciting, but also challenging. In practical terms, the problem is often one of where simply to even begin in writing-up a project of such magnitude. There may be no obvious starting point, no clear way 'around the garden' when traversing comparative terrain. Of course, a sense of paralysis or 'writer's block' can afflict all academics from time to time, but it may manifest in an especially acute manner for those wrestling with the challenges of comparative interpretive research. The blank page can be even more intimidating than usual. Our first rules of thumb, therefore, advocate strategies for getting things down on paper initially, in the hope and faith that a structure will emerge in the creative mess that results.

Rule #1: Don't Wait for the Muse to Arrive

In the face of endless choice, the key is just to get words on the page. You cannot sit there and wait for the muse to arrive. Writing is the day job. It is a craft. There is no substitute for learning by doing. So, though we have often given it ample thought in advance, there is no need to have settled on a final answer for how the material will be organised and presented as a first step before writing. In our experience, this initial plan never works out anyway. Brainstorming and plotting how to organise an account is but a stone's throw from procrastination. We find it helps to just get stuck in.

The easiest way to overcome paralysis is to start with tales from the field – we mean here not just descriptions of fieldwork, but writing from fieldwork sites to capture the energy and inspiration of the experience (see Chapter 5 especially). Writing is not a discrete activity that takes place upon returning from the field. Writing is research and research is writing. The two activities are coterminous. In the initial stages, we find it useful to start by putting the most interesting quotes or vignettes on the blank page. We sort these into provisional themes and categories, seeing how the data fits. All of a sudden, the page is no longer blank! Once we start to write short explanations of why the quotes are interesting, and how they relate to other quotes on the page, things start to take shape. The numbers of words will quickly swell and themes will emerge. The chances are this will result in too many words. Little by little, we can revise the prose, whittle it down and make it more coherent. But this process requires the discipline of writing every day.

Of course, no one succeeds in writing *absolutely* every day. Teaching, administrative work, family, even – heaven forfend – recreation can get in the way. A little determination and a *soupçon* of planning can remove some of the obstacles. One professor with four children was head of department and increasingly frustrated with this workload. The dean and the professor came up with a partial solution. The dean found a small room in another building with no phone, only a computer and no name on the door. The professor worked in that room from 09:00 to 11:00 every day and became head of department only after 11:00. It gave the professor on average about ten hours a week of research time. Of course, the professor could have worked at home or locked the door in the department. However, the different room in the different building with set hours provided a supportive, disciplined framework for writing. Another professor was an early riser, with grown up children who worked from 06:00 to 09:00 at home before coming into the university to become the dean (see also Wildavsky 2010: 7–8). Everyone can devise their own preferred work pattern. On days when we did not feel like writing, we compiled and checked the bibliography, made sure we had applied the style sheet correctly, added quotes that might be useful, and so on. Also, especially given the incessant demand for more publication, a smaller, side project to your labour of love can be a great help. There are two reasons. When your main project confounds you, and a break from it is essential, you can still write. Also, labours of love take time. Side projects enable you to publish while labouring.

Psychologists interested in creativity increasingly talk about the importance of 'flow' when a person is fully immersed in a task to the exclusion of virtually everything else around them (see Perry 1999). The effect is similar to what athletes experience when they are 'in the zone', when the mind and body are so focused they feel they could go on forever; it seems effortless. Writing can be like that. We have sat down after breakfast and, before we knew it, it is time for dinner. When in the zone, fingers flying over the keys, words appear as if by magic. Ideas spring unbidden. However, writing in the zone is rare, and it cannot be scheduled. All too often, writing is hard work, messy, confusing and intimidating. Practising by getting words on the page is key to developing a rhythm for writing.

Rule #2: Use Writing as a Form of Thinking

This rule of thumb is, in essence, an injunction to embrace a practice of writing that becomes patterned, natural and automatic. But the corollary of treating writing as a craft – as the day job – means it should not demand or require (too much) thinking in advance. We do not need to fully map out where we are going before we start. We stress again, mulling it over too much can be a recipe for paralysis. Now we explain why. The reason we do not need to work everything out neatly in advance is because writing itself is such a powerful prompt for creative thought.

We are not, of course, the first to note the relationship between writing and thinking. The idea that getting it down on paper aids the creative process is true for all kinds of research – indeed for authorship of all kinds – is a fairly well-worn staple of established 'how to write' guides. We do not claim it as an original *aperçu*. Our purpose here is to describe and show how it is especially crucial for thinking through how to organise and structure comparative interpretive research. We do so through a story.

When Rhodes sat down in his study in Tasmania in 2008 to write up the fieldwork for the book that became *Everyday Life in British Government* (Rhodes 2011), he was in a mild panic. He had been an 'artificial person' (Wolgast 1992: 1), or Head of Department then Director/Dean, for five years. Daily life was a procession of committee and one-to-one meetings, which encouraged a short attention span. He wondered if he could sit at the computer and concentrate for eight hours a day. Then there were the interviews and the fieldwork notebooks, comparing three different departments all with their own idiosyncrasies. On day 1, they seemed a formless mess, more intimidating than informative. His organising principle was starting at the top of the pile and working his way down. He put the material in date order and started reading, making notes as he went along. He could start writing also because he knew he would use the interpretive theory he had developed with Mark Bevir. Its basic concepts of beliefs, practices, traditions and dilemmas helped to structure the first read through. He knew his methods were a variant on classical ethnography. He could write the theory and methods chapter. But what to do about the fieldwork? There was no list of chapters beyond that invented for the book proposal. There was no plan. Only themes and topics identified from reading and rereading the fieldwork. He wrote it in sections. The first section was a day in the life of a public servant because the public servant's diary structured the description. As he wrote, as he tried to stand in the shoes of the minister and his public servants, themes became plain. One observation was the practice of some ministers of avoiding decisions for the pomp and circumstance of office. It led to the notion of 'the appearance of rule' as a public exhibition of governmental authority. Some metaphors were revealing such as describing the entourage around the minister as a 'court'. The analogy with a jigsaw is relevant again. He was putting pieces together while looking for the bigger picture. He started with the observations and tried to find the most likely explanation of why people did what they did. At times, he plotted backwards, trying to work out how he got to where he was. At times, his writing 'plan' was like M. C. Esher's lithograph of the continuous Penrose staircase.

In sum, Rhodes practised abductive puzzling *through* writing, and a natural 'structure' to the monograph came together. It wasn't magic. It was hard work. But the point is that Rhodes would never have arrived at these comparative insights if he had just kept staring at his data until an ideal structure or organising device leapt out at him. Just getting on with it was key.

Rule #3: Stylise Your Findings

Much of what we have said thus far can be boiled down to a pithy phrase: 'shut up and write'. We stress this because of the twin threats of procrastination and paralysis. But, obviously, we cannot spend all our time writing. Aside from those rare moments 'in the zone', it is arduous work. There can be severely diminishing returns from extended sessions. In our experience – and the available evidence for most people (see Swales and Feak 2004) – having a relatively short, regular and scheduled writing pattern is much more profitable than going on occasional writing binges. So what to do when we have stopped producing text for the day? This is when we find it useful to come back from a break with an editor's pen, and consciously work to *stylise* the findings.

The logic here is that writing is an intense task and we can become lost in the detail of the stories we are trying to tell. As such, this process is especially important if the structure emerging resembles a case-by-case, contextual account. As researchers, our inclination is to tell the full story of each case. But comparative interpretive research requires stylisation. Much of the audience does not care intrinsically about the case. The task is to focus on telling them why they should care. Taking a break, and assuming a change in role from writer to editor, can help to see the wood through the trees. It serves to solidify and clarify the emergent structure.

Taking on this task can even be something as simple as installing sub-headings that capture comparative categories. In a PhD thesis or book, each chapter will be between 8,000 and 10,000 words. This means at least four to five main sections, each of which can be broken down into smaller sub-sections. As a general guide, we like to have a sub-heading *at least* every two to four pages. In an article we have them even more frequently – every two to four paragraphs. At times this will feel somewhat forced or artificial, but crafting the structure so that it begins to feel more and more authentic is a key part of the creative process. By necessity it will highlight the sections of text that are superfluous because they will not be relevant to the other cases. It will also help identify gaps in the account because sections that are important to one case will be missing from others.

Naturally, alternating between writer and editor can be disheartening. What seemed like pearls of wisdom one day can seem rather less shiny and alluring the next day. Often, we spend all morning writing 1,500 words only to realise later in the day that 1,000 of them are not relevant for the piece at hand. It can feel like taking three steps forward, two steps back. But we try to keep the offcuts – they may be useful for another day. Rhodes's continuing side project on the craft of public administration benefits from such offcuts. The main project is a comparative study of ministers, but there are many asides about the relationship between politicians and public servants. These asides often get cut and go into a dump file to be used on the craft project (see Rhodes 2016: 642). In any case, we find this strategy helpful in the slow and painful iteration towards a clear and convincing structure.

Addressing the Dilemma of Style

Rule #4: Be Both Linear and Evocative

Different traditions prize different styles of prose or modes of presentation. In the humanist tradition, there is appetite for rich descriptive detail and creative evocation of the context under examination. In the naturalist tradition, the format and formula is often tighter, more prescriptive and more linear. Attempting to write for both of these worlds is difficult. Indeed, specialists in one world often find it hard to *read* the work of specialists in another.

As interpretivists, our personal inclination is towards evocation. To evoke is to call forth images of people and places; to persuade readers that they know these people and have been to these places: 'the mode of storytelling is akin to the novel or the biography and thus fractures the boundaries that normally separate social science from literature' (Ellis and Bochner 2000: 744). The authorial voice is present. The text is written in the first person. The author is as much subject as the ostensible subjects. There is considerable scope for textual experimentation. Our aim when writing-up fieldwork is 'to master, explain, grasp' while 'caring and empathizing' for our research subjects, and recognising that we are all actors in the same play (cf. Ellis and Bochner 2006: 431). We explore the relationship between data and concepts. The ultimate goal is to wed storytelling with analysis in a way that is artful, creative, engaging and above all, evocative.

However, our personal preferences do not necessarily conform to the performance metrics of modern academia. Indeed, there is increasingly an expectation that, especially for interpretivists, we must write for multiple audiences. Like it or not, positivist approaches represent the mainstream in most social science disciplines if not area studies. The outlets that publish this sort of work dominate. Impact factor metrics and perceived rankings of 'top journals' and 'best presses' feed in to the calculations associated with job searches, performance appraisal regimes, and tenure and promotion committees. Doing comparative interpretive research, we suggest, offers an approach that can produce the big theoretical claims essential to publication in a mainstream journal. However, in doing so, we confront a clash of styles. There is a standard template of what constitutes good research practice and it leaves little space for creative flourishes.

This dilemma of style was ever present even in the writing of this book, which itself is as good an example as any of taking an unorthodox set of messages and trying to sell them to a mainstream audience. Rhodes was the established professor and he wrote mainly books for university presses that tolerated his stylistic improvisations. Boswell and Corbett were at earlier stages in their career. They felt under pressure from heads of department, deans and promotions committees to conform to the mainstream template. How could we advise colleagues to experiment with their writing styles when such experimentation could damage their career prospects? Yet the point of the book is to challenge the mainstream on theory, method and writing-up. How did we resolve the dilemma? We were pragmatic. We make it clear that there is a dilemma between cultivating a distinctive voice and writing for a template. We freely admit that we compromise and follow the mainstream template at least some of the time. After all, without a job, we will change nothing. Yet we remain committed to the belief that there are many valid ways of studying politics and just as many ways of writing-up our studies. The abiding challenge is one of working out which way to write, and for whom, in practice.

Rule #5: Experiment with Form and Genre

Like all creative enterprises, it can be a difficult one to get started. One especially generative and productive way to start 'getting it down' on paper is to experiment with different modes or forms of presentation – to borrow ideas from other literary inspirations in order to work through key ideas as they emerge.

An obvious place to start is with academic writing that is seminal or inspiring for the research at hand. We find this especially useful when thinking about how to package our research for a mainstream audience. We find a lot of work in 'top' journals – both the methodologically technical and the theoretically dense – borderline impenetrable. But of course not all of it fits this stereotype. And we admire especially interpretive researchers who are able to bridge the divide and speak to, and have a big influence on, a mainstream audience. Boswell, for instance, takes particular inspiration from contemporary authors like Cramer (2012, 2016) and Soss (2002; Soss and Schram 2007). They are interpretivists who have successfully communicated insights from rich fieldwork to mainstream audiences, and had a profound effect on how scholars now understand and study popular resentment and alienation from the state. Rhodes found useful guidance for writing his books not only in the work of anthropologists such as Clifford Geertz (1973) but also in such bestsellers as Kate Fox (2004), *Watching the English: The Hidden Rules of English Behaviour*. For sure, many of these authors write for academic journals that, while still highly readable, are far more economical with words and less evocative than their monographs. Although we do not know them personally, we imagine they would choose not to write for such journals if given carte blanche. Yet occasionally constraining and channelling Big-C creativity in this way seems a small price to pay for speaking to and influencing a large audience.

Having models in our own or adjacent fields is useful, but we can also look much further afield for inspiration. In fact, the skills of writing-up fieldwork can equally blur into the skills of writing fiction, especially when we seek to *evoke* the everyday life and its dilemmas of others. Consequently, there can be as much to learn from the art of the novel as from the dry guides on how to write a thesis, book or article. Recreational reading can be an important source of inspiration. Travel writing can be analogous to writing-up comparative interpretive research. The travel writer moves from place to place, a perpetual stranger attempting to render a context meaningful, to both themselves and their audience. They learn much about local dilemmas, beliefs and practices by talking to people and observing their everyday life. However, their explanation of these dilemmas, beliefs and practices is always informed by why they are travelling, where they have come from and where they are going to. They convey their experience in the same way: the food smells or tastes like somewhere else, the buildings are grander or more dilapidated than they had expected and so on. They sprinkle the text with literary and musical allusions – what they are listening to or reading at the time – to leaven the mix. They offer personal anecdotes – they are present in the text and not an impersonal, detached commentator. They write in the first person and the active voice. For everyone, good writing involves making these choices.

Travel writing invokes the stylistic motif of a journey, but often that motif will not fit a research story. Instead ask yourself how the author tells their story. What narrative devices do they employ? For example, most crime authors sustain the reader's interest by using 'incidentals'. Inspector Salvo Montalbano is a gourmand and Andrea Camilleri litters the books with references to Sicilian food. What is the plot – how does the story unfold? In other words, look at the book's skeleton. For example, in Agatha Christie's *The Murder of Roger Ackroyd*, the narrator is the murderer, although the reader does not know it until the end. It will take only a few minutes to make a few notes on how the author told the story. By performing this autopsy, any author will become more aware of the options available.

Rule #6: Be Flexible in How You Talk about Your Work

Much is written about the need for authors to have a distinct voice or style. Indeed, Aaron Wildavsky, ever the wordsmith, devotes much of his *Craft-ways* to discussing ways to find this unique voice. We demur somewhat from his traditional advice. We think it is possible, even fruitful, to have different voices, or at least different registers of voice, depending on the audience. The successful 'translators' of interpretive insight we discussed earlier are proof. The key to doing so is a willingness to be flexible.

We have already outlined the need to employ narrative devices self-consciously. Here the emphasis is on how to alter the narrative device to suit different audiences and outlets. Hayden White invites us to consider the many modes of emplotment; that is, ways of assembling a series of historical events into a story with a plot. He identifies four 'modes of emplotment': romance, tragedy, comedy and satire. Each mode has its associated tropes or figures of speech used for artistic effect. The choice of mode and tropes prefigures both the story (and its plot) and, therefore, the explanation (White 1973: chapter 1; and White 1987: chapter 2; see also Barthes 1970). Lacking a shared technical language, politics and history rely on familiar figures of speech (or ordinary language) to create meaning; on the metaphorical use of words. Historians (and political scientists) 'constitute their subjects as possible objects of narrative representation by the very language they use to describe them' (White 1987: 94–95). Booker (2005) identifies seven basic plots that could be used in each mode of emplotment: overcoming the monster, rags to riches, the quest, voyage and return, comedy, tragedy and rebirth. The 'quest' and 'voyage and return' are well suited to fieldwork.

Each way of telling the tale will reveal only a partial truth. What are the choices? As van Maanen (2010: 241) comments 'literary practices are terra incognita' yet political scientists need to become self-conscious practitioners of a literary craft that embraces literary experimentation (Hammersley and Atkinson 2007: chapter 9). Therefore, we need more and better ways to tell of our research findings (van Maanen 1988: 2, 8 and 14),

Van Maanen (1988: 2, 8 and 14; and 2010) identifies five ways of telling tales: realist, confessional, impressionist, poststructural and advocacy.

Realist tales are dispassionate, third-person documentary accounts of everyday life that 'represent' the subject's standpoint. Comparative interpretive researchers are typically uncomfortable with realism. But needs must. Reviewers for mainstream journals expect, often demand, realism. There is limited room for manoeuvre.

The characteristics of a *confessional* account are more intuitive in the comparative interpretive research endeavour. This account is an autobiographical, personalised story, which tells the tale from the fieldworker's perspective; and aims for naturalness and getting it right in the end. Confessional tales are first person and anecdotal (van Maanen 1988: chapter 4 and p. 79).

As the name implies, *impressionist* tales fit impressionistic analysis. Such tales have a fragmented treatment of theory and method, because they focus on characterisation and drama (van Maanen 1988: 103–106). They 'highlight the episodic, complex and ambivalent realities that are frozen and perhaps made too pat by realist or confessional conventions'. We forsake the realist 'doctrine of immaculate perception' (van Maanen 1988: 74), but court the danger of succumbing to the 'diary disease' (Geertz 1988: 90) where the narrator's voice is dominant.

Poststructural tales' main characteristics are 'textual innovation, disorder, the wavering of meaning, and open-endedness'. Reality is 'treated as a fragile social construction' (van Maanen 2010: 248). He concludes that 'poststructural tales are inevitably inconclusive', and suggest we see them as fieldwork 'from another planet' (van Mannen 2010: 249).

Advocacy tales have missionary zeal. The aim is to right the evils of the world and the prose is 'moral and normative' (Van Maanen 2010: 250).

In identifying these five styles, we do not advocate any one mode, trope or plot. Clearly, there is no one way of reporting from the field. There is no necessary connection between impressionistic analysis and impressionistic writing. For the mainstream journal article, it may be wise to adopt realist writing conventions. We seek to show only that the craft of writing is paramount and there is an extensive menu from which to choose. Also, we insist that the reader knows what the writer is doing and why. If they are advocating for (say) a community group, it is incumbent on the author to make his or her allegiances clear so the reader can take that into account.

It is hard enough being a specialist in a single country let alone several. It is also hard enough being on top of current work in a single discipline given the amount published. Now, on top of that, we expect researchers to be an author; to understand narrative techniques, to invent plot lines and to indulge in characterisation. Jokingly, van Maanen (2010: 241) suggests that, when confronted by this literary challenge, 'it is best to imitate the ostrich and not look'. Our point is that there is value in writing that is relatively free from technical jargon, uses everyday language, is not burdened with arcane discussions of methods and 'continues to carry a slight literary air compared to other forms of social science writing' (van Maanen 2010: 251). Pragmatically, for our articles, we adopt the style favoured by journals. For the more expansive book, there are a greater array of choices and styles.

Rule #7: Practice the Art of Translation

Thus far, we have mainly discussed writing articles, chapters and books for an academic readership. There are other audiences, notably, the public, schools, and practitioners. These audiences compound further the dilemma of style. Here, we discuss the core activity of the 'art of translation'

(Flinders 2013). Rhodes had an early introduction to this craft in his first job at the Institute of Local Government Studies (INLOGOV), University of Birmingham. The Institute taught long and short management courses for local government officers and conducted consultancy research for government. We were encouraged to write for our local government audience as well as academic journals. So, Rhodes cut his teeth on the *Local Government Chronicle, Municipal Review* and *Municipal Journal* as well as academic journals such as the *Journal of Common Market Studies* and *Public Administration*. Because the local government journals were run like newspapers, subeditors revised his work and taught him how to write for them. No such luck with his Home Office consultancy report on *The Councillor, Information and Urban Deprivation* (July 1975). It is a good example of how not to write for a government department.

Rhodes wrote the report using systems theory to organise the data. Chapter 2 provides a 'framework of analysis', which is a conventional input–output communication model of decision making in local government. After that sentence, it will come as no surprise that the report contains such gems as:

The information retained is seen as sufficient by the decision makers for making a decision. This decision contains within it (implicitly or explicitly) –

  i. a definition of the problem which is congruent with the expectations, interests and values of the interacting groups.
 ii. a statement of priorities in terms of (a) the differential attention paid to different sources of information and (b) the bargains agreed between interacting groups each emphasising different value premises ordered differently.
iii. a statement of the course of action with the greatest probability of not disrupting the relationship between (a) the organisation and its environment and (b) the several internal groups. (Rhodes 1975: 14)

This extract has so many faults, it is hard to know where to start. The style is academic, unsuitable for a practitioner readership. The prose is unrelentingly abstract. Rhodes did not provide any concrete examples either here or in the following text. He employed the passive voice, which reinforces the abstract, detached voice of the author. Readers would be hard pressed to know he wrote about the emotive issue of poverty in British cities. Even worse, the report concluded with the unhelpful observation that 'the problem is relatively clear. The solutions, even partial ones, remain obscure'.

The disdain of the civil servant on reading the report was palpable (and justified). Rhodes has not worked for the Home Office again! That matters not. The point is that from the beginning, with varying degrees of success, INLOGOV taught him how to write for different audiences.

The ability to write in several ways is referred to by Flinders (2013) as the 'art of translation'. The phrase refers to translating academic articles, books and chapters into accessible pieces for professional journals, teaching material for school and university students, and discussion pieces for newspapers and social media. This approach ensures that every academic output (that is, first phase writing) is automatically translated into some form of practitioner paper such as a report for a government department or charity (that is, second phase) before finally being translated into a much shorter and accessible output for the public, such as a newspaper article or blog (that is, third phase). Moreover, to reach many audiences in the twenty-first century, 'publication' covers social media, podcasts and other visual media.

The Dilemma of Substance

We return now to the final dilemma – one that persists through all aspects of the comparative interpretive dilemma: managing the depth–breadth trade-off. This trade-off inherent in conducting comparative interpretive research comes to a head when writing-up. As scholars, we want to render the stories and experiences of the everyday lives we encountered as authentic to the participants in our research. However, we also want to make plausible conjectures that contribute in a significant way to the academic audiences in which our work is situated. There is no easy answer to this dilemma, just as the pursuit of perfect writing is futile. Our last rules of thumb provide some guidance for managing the tension.

Rule #8: Hustle and Recycle

The most obvious approach to managing the depth–breadth trade-off, particularly when aligned to a contextual case-by-case approach, is to operate a dual strategy – write up papers on each case and combine them in a single book manuscript later. Take Maarten Hajer's (2009) path-breaking *Authoritative Governance* as an example. In the broader monograph, Hajer draws on three different case studies – the response to the assassination of Theo van Gogh in the Netherlands; the planning process around the rebuilding of Ground Zero in New York; and the establishment of the Food Standards Agency in the UK – to build an account of how authority in contemporary democratic governance is 'performed' across an intricate array of stages, settings and scripts. Hajer's comparison is an excellent example of what we are talking about in this book, although he prefers the term 'crisis' to dilemma in his brief justification of this unorthodox design. He had already published each of the case studies elsewhere as single-case papers, in the process demonstrating sufficient mastery of each context for more main-stream public administration and public policy journals. The book – though still with a prestige press – opened up greater creativity in linking and drawing themes across the breadth of cases.

Hajer's approach is the most common way to manage the tension between a broad sweep and a narrow depth. But it is far from the only way. We are big advocates of hustling and recycling, using material for different purposes to communicate (either depth or breadth) to different audiences.

Recycling is sometimes looked down on as a form of 'self-plagiarism'. This notion is an oxymoron. We cannot steal that which we wrote. We are not using someone else's words. We are reusing our own words, and it is a legitimate use with two provisos. First, we must get the publisher's permission to avoid infringing copyright. Most publishers have no problem with such requests, provided it is for an extract and not the complete text. Second, we must not claim the work is new. Any recycling should contain an acknowledgement to the original article. With apologies to Tom Lehrer for this modification of the words to his song 'Lobachevsky', 'self-plagiarize, self-plagiarize let none of your work escape their eyes', because the important point is not the recycling but the endeavour to reach as many readers as possible. Given the call for relevant research, such recycling is exactly what heads of department, Deans, even governments want to see. The expectation is that researchers will offer their findings and insights to a broad and diverse set of audiences not just to a professional, niche audience.

The goal of reaching as many readers as possible is made easier in comparative interpretive research because this type of research automatically has multiple audiences: the audience interested in the substantive topic and the audience interested in the geographical location in which the research was conducted. Corbett, for example, used his work on the Pacific to contribute to debates in the Area Studies literature (e.g. Corbett 2012; Corbett and Shiu 2014). He also wrote articles for different political science audiences: on political leadership (Corbett 2013a, 2015b; Corbett and Wood 2013); political parties (Corbett 2015c); gender (Corbett and Liki 2015); religion (Corbett 2013b), etc. Each of these were a small section in the book he wrote on Pacific politicians. In the articles, he drew on the material that was left on the cutting room floor to expand on different substantive topics. One such intervention, on the effects of state size on the practice of democratic leadership (Corbett 2015b), led to his subsequent work on small states, with Wouter Veenendaal. They worked in a similar way; they wrote a book and several spin-off articles (e.g. articles: Corbett and Veenendaal 2016; Corbett, Veenendaal and Ugyel 2017; Veenendaal and Corbett 2015; and book: Corbett and Veenendaal 2018).

While this strategy sounds an attractive way of fleshing out a CV, it is also demanding in its own way. As a rule of thumb, top Area Studies journals have a much higher empirical bar than disciplinary journals. Corbett, for example, has been rejected by such journals because he had not done enough in-depth empirical work, but he never faced that type of criticism in disciplinary journals. By contrast, disciplinary journals are likely to have a much higher bar in terms of theoretical innovation and the justification for case selection. In both cases, as discussed at length above, know your audience and adapt your style, language and mode of presentation to suit the conventions of each outlet.

Rule #9: Share Your Work Early and Widely

If hustling and recycling is the end goal or overarching strategy for managing the depth–breadth trade-off, then there is also a question about how you develop and produce outputs that will be acceptable to these different audiences along the way.

Once the first draft is complete, do not be precious. Give the manuscript a public airing. Get family and friends as well as colleagues to read it through. The former will point out whether it is in English. We hope the latter will spot academic weaknesses. Even better, persuade a well-published senior colleague to act as an 'informal' referee.

Professional association conferences and smaller sub-disciplinary workshops obviously present other opportunities to share work early and widely. These can be hit and miss in practice, but there is little to lose (and potentially much to gain) from airing work in such forums.

More important, we find, is the feedback of a select few colleagues and friends – trusted readers who we always use as a first round of review. This arrangement can be ad hoc (and it is always quid pro quo), but it can be formalised as well. Corbett and Boswell are part of a network of scholars who do broadly similar work. Half a dozen of the group meet twice a year to provide a first round of peer review on articles (or chapters, or book or grant proposals). The format is: one hour per paper; the author gets two minutes to introduce their paper and from then on they are not allowed to defend it, only ask for clarification; two discussants mimic sympathetic and hostile reviewers. These reviews are followed by general discussion of not only the paper's strengths and weaknesses but also how to revise it for the given target journal. The benefit is each paper receives intense, high-quality comments. There is a further benefit. The cast of people attending changes each time, and there is often (and we can deliberately invite and encourage) a mix of specialists *and* generalists. In comparative interpretive work, this mix is essential. We need to know not only that our account rings true to context specialists but also that our conjectures are plausible and meaningful to generalists. The cost, of course, is that each author has to read and comment on five other papers. Yet this ostensible chore has the added benefit of exposing us to different styles, genres and approaches to writing. The event itself entails lots of 'talking shop' about the practice of writing and aims and challenges of publishing. It is collegial, and energising fun. Corbett and Boswell did not invent the model – they emulated a group of International Political Economy scholars – but it has greatly improved their work and their enjoyment of academic life.

Rule #10: Seek Input from the Field

The expression writing 'for' different audiences is potentially misleading. We can also write 'with' the subjects of our research; we can share our findings with them and incorporate their comments in the final version. The buzz word for such cooperation is 'co-production'. We prefer the phrase 'fusion of horizons'; that is, the search for an understanding arising from 'negotiation between oneself and one's partner in the hermeneutical dialogue' in which an agreement 'means establishing a common framework or "horizon"' (Malpass 2013; see also Gadamer 1960). It is consistent with our interpretive approach. It is also an immensely valuable part of writing, as we recover the stories told by our research subjects. We systematise these accounts, telling our version of their stories. Then we ask the subjects of our fieldwork to read and comment on the story; that is, we recount our version of their story back to them. Jointly, we review the story, mapping points of agreement and disagreement and searching for a fusion of horizons. That fusion is often elusive, and there will be several remaining points of disagreement. A fusion of horizons covers both agreement and where we agree to disagree. We report both outcomes in the final version of the story and, with true authorial majesty, we offer our explanation of the disagreements. This sharing adds to the plausibility of our account because it provides corroboration by the subjects and an external check on the consistency of our arguments.

For example, Rhodes circulated a draft of *Everyday Life in British Government* to all the permanent secretaries and ministers quoted in the book for their comments. With their permission, he included their replies in the final chapter (see Rhodes 2011: 303–305). We reproduce their replies below to show that they engaged seriously with the text.

I have no problems with the text you sent. It is all suitably anonymised, so causes no problems. Interesting six years on to wonder whether anything is changing. I think PPSs stay a bit longer (2 years is more common). It is increasingly difficult to persuade some of our 'high-fliers' to regard Private Office as an essential part of their education. This is partly because of the reputation for long and unsocial hours; but partly because there are so many attractions – fast streamers these days get the chance to have a secondment to another department and/or voluntary body. And promotion offers come quickly. Otherwise I think there is much truth in the portrait, except that it is inevitably very influenced by personality – on both the PPS and the ministerial sides.

So much for the good news. The disagreements were more instructive. One Minister was borderline splenetic:

I am afraid I was completely dismayed to read your draft. You assured me – and my permanent secretary – that this was a serious piece of research and that the participants would not be identified or identifiable. In fact, both I and the Department are clearly recognisable and as a result, I believe that many of your quotations and observations will inevitably be used in a way that neither of us intended, or believed you intended, when we agreed to participate. The result, I am afraid, is extremely unfair to our departmental colleagues. I am therefore not prepared to give my permission either for my name to be used or for the quotes to be attributed.

To be fair, after reading a later draft with the offending passages revised, the Minister conceded 'I'm glad to say that I found it much more interesting and substantial than I'd expected'.

Rhodes's version of the story did not convince everyone.

There is no attempt to locate the scenes in wider contexts of managerial and societal change; no comparison with equally challenging pressures on senior people in equivalent positions in the private sector, other parts of the public sector, or big charities; no discussion of the external drivers of change, e.g. text messages and emails, greater openness, the web, 24-hour news, developing management theories and styles; indeed the whole flavour is that those observed are in their own, separate, world with its own, separate, pressures. I don't think that is right, and I suspect that similar observation of leaders in other sectors would throw up some very similar conclusions.

These remarks are accurate. The book does not document the changes but shows how the civil service and ministers coped with these changes. The previous quote displays the managerial cast of mind. Others were more traditional and sanguine in their outlook:

It's interesting re-reading this several years on, after doing another Permanent Secretary job and a year after retirement from the civil service. It captures the sense of 'village' at the top of Departments. It inevitably presents a snapshot, and rather different themes could have come out if the fieldwork in any one Department had been done at a different time; but that doesn't invalidate it, and the overall impression seems to me fair. At the risk of stating the obvious, the atmosphere in this village depends crucially on the personalities of the key players, and the degree of trust between them. What has changed since the fieldwork was done? There's more emphasis now on the corporate (i.e. civil service-wide) role of Permanent Secretaries, with aspects of this featuring in the performance objectives they agree with the Cabinet Secretary. And it's harder to attract high-fliers into Private Office jobs.

In short, Rhodes's correspondents engaged constructively with his text and by so doing enable the reader to put the author's interpretation in context. It is clear the book is Rhodes' interpretation of what the public servants and ministers think they are doing. Others have used the same approach and had beneficial, if at times confronting, experiences (see 't Hart 2007). Nonetheless, such criticism improves the manuscript. However, it is not without its dangers. For some, consultations over the draft manuscript become a nightmare of conflict and delay because the mirror held up to either individuals or their organisation is unflattering (see, Burns 1977: ix–xviii on the British Broadcasting Corporation; and Punch 1986: chapter 3 and p. 77 on the 'progressive' Dartington Hall School in Devon).

The broader point, however, is that seeking input from fieldwork respondents can be a vital check on a late copy of a manuscript. We suspect this statement is accurate for all kinds of research. It is especially important in attending to the breadth–depth tension in comparative interpretive research when attempting to make plausible conjectures of broad applicability. It is a good way of seeking reassurance that the comparative write-up rings true across the actors and settings in the study.

Conclusion

Writing-up is when we are forced to wrestle with (and against) the competing traditions of the single idiographic case and the large-N generalisability in the most exposed and painful manner. There can be a sense of paralysis about where to even start in seeking to present adequately a coherent set of findings in the face of the overwhelming messiness of a complex, multifaceted research project. There is a further dilemma around which genre or academic 'voice' to engage in: to be, at one extreme, the detached comparativist making a broad theoretical contribution via a linear account or, at the other, the engaged interpretivist telling evocative stories of idiographic human experience. And writing-up further reinforces the tension, underlying all aspects of a comparative interpretive research project, between providing a sufficiently 'thick description' on the one hand, while simultaneously seeking to cover multiple cases, on the other.

In this chapter, we have wrestled with these dilemmas of writing-up comparative interpretive research. But we certainly have not resolved them. We hope that our rules of thumb will provide guidance along the way. We remain resolute that comparative interpretive research is worth pursuing. But reflecting on the challenges of writing-up reminds us that it is not easy. Perhaps more even than typical academic endeavours, it requires a thick skin, a phlegmatic attitude and a healthy dose of pragmatism. We turn in our conclusion to reflect on these characteristics as we sum up the key messages from the book.

8   Retrospective

Three white men holding permanent academic posts, one a distinguished professor in a research-intensive position, the other two younger scholars juggling the competing demands of teaching, service and raising small children, sit down to write a book. It sounds like the start of bad joke but it is too serious for that. It introduces the subject of *professional reflexivity*. We faced several dilemmas in writing this book. We reflect on them because reflexivity is central to our craft.

Reflexivity is inescapable and our reflections are not original. We suggest that none of the dilemmas we discuss here are unique, even if the combination and our experience of them is distinctive. We would expect many readers to be able to compare our dilemmas with their own, and learn something new from engaging in such a process. It will help us to think how the comparative intuition might become an explicit method for social scientists working in the interpretive tradition.

The Dilemma of Different Audiences

The first dilemma we grappled with concerned the audience(s) for the book. Each of us had our pet targets: Boswell wanted to thumb his nose at journal reviewers and editors who sought fuller and fuller justifications for his comparative case selection. Corbett was still jousting with the area studies scholars with whom he did his PhD and post-doctoral work. Rhodes was continuing a decades' long debate with his contemporaries on the limits to political science. Collectively, we wanted to say something that resonated beyond the narrow confines of these professional arenas. Specifically, we wanted to write a book that all of those scholars working in an interpretive tradition, who wanted to make comparative claims, could lean on to justify the unlikeliest of case selections or writing styles. We imagined a somewhat anarchic guide to research practice that could aid scholars seeking to be creative and find out new things.

But, we wondered if we were still being too narrow – was our focus on interpretive political science still playing to our home court advantage in the UK and Europe in particular? Could we say something that would feed into fast-developing debates in the USA about comparative interpretive research and qualitative data collection (see Elman, Kapiszewski and Lupia 2018; Isaac 2015; Lupia and Elman 2014)? Also, the question of comparison is of broader relevance beyond political sciences. Other disciplines grapple with making the creative links across contexts that we make. No single book can be all things to all readers. In the end, we focused mainly on the audience that we know best – UK and European political science, and scholars working in the interpretive tradition. We hope that readers on the other side of the Atlantic and elsewhere in the world will nevertheless find aspects of this book useful for the questions they seek to answer. Likewise, we will be delighted if the book finds an audience beyond our discipline of political science. Certainly the headline arguments should resonate across genres, even if the examples are largely our own.

Both of these dilemmas have informed the text, including our decisions about chapter structure, content and style. They have produced a multitude of small-d dilemmas that we have, consciously or unconsciously, sought to solve against the backdrop of competing deadlines, busy schedules and family commitments. For example, the book is essentially linear – approach, case selection, fieldwork, analysis and writing-up – yet we argue for impressionistic analysis and creative intuition. We chose to use a linear structure to persuade a mainstream audience rather than telling a postmodernist tale. We agreed to disagree when it came to the rules of thumb on writing-up – Rhodes wanted to thumb his nose at the norms of mainstream journals while Boswell and Corbett wanted to provide guidance for early career colleagues whose priority when reading this book is likely to be how to get published in a top journal. In the end, we attempted to do both.

None of these solutions are perfect or seamless. They continue to puzzle us. In this sense, we are essentially similar to the people whose lives we study.

The Dilemma of Who We Are

When Rhodes began his academic career, the fact that he was a white male would have been assumed, and so there would have been no distinct dilemma in our writing this book. Much has changed over the last five decades, and the explicit recognition that positionality and privilege fundamentally shape all scholarly work is one of the most salient, which is why we have wrestled with how to approach it here.

What makes us uncomfortable is that our approach to decentring by comparing dilemmas is explicitly an attempt to render the exotic familiar and the familiar exotic. This move is out of the ordinary. It is more common for scholars to defend the unfamiliar and the exotic by highlighting that there are different, often irreconcilable, ways of seeing and living in the world. They would argue also that only somebody finely attuned to these differences, and indeed speaking from within a particular community, can appreciate the subtleties. This strand of scholarship seeks to highlight the way power and privilege render some ways of living and acting in the world more valuable than others.

To compound our dilemma, the inspirational figures we draw on, aside from our research participants and collaborators, are also privileged white men: Clifford Geertz, F.G. Bailey and Benedict Anderson. They too sought to defend the unfamiliar and exotic, but their method was to render it intelligible to the uninitiated. To translate, across time and space, by providing analytical tools that brought otherwise irreconcilable peoples, places and cultures into conversation through common questions such as how is a sense of nation created out of otherwise disparate communities? Or, how do leaders win the supporters and allies to enact change? By rendering the exotic familiar they sought to pluralise the academic field by adding new stories and perspectives. Rather than seeking to defend so-called traditional societies against the homogenising tendencies of imperialist domination, they sought to highlight that they were not unfamiliar – that the 'West' is not as modern as it thinks it is – and therefore could be treated as equals.

Obviously, given the nature of this book, our sympathies and normative preferences are broadly aligned with making the exotic familiar. Still, nagging doubt remains. Does focusing on dilemmas allow us to address power imbalances, to identify inequalities, to give voice to the silent? We cannot definitively answer 'Yes!' We think it can. We hope it will. But, in truth, the proof will be in the type of work this book, and its approach to the study of the social and political world, inspires. We have written it the only way we could write it – from our perspective based on our experience. It is the first stone, not the last word. Our hope is that others will challenge and refine our ideas through trial, error and practice, and in doing so assuage our anxiety. But, at the same time, because the underlying dilemma is about how to approach power asymmetries that are, to some extent, always present in human interactions, our suspicion is that all scholars will and probably need to reflect continuously on how who they are shapes what they say, and why and how they say it.

The Dilemma of Dilemmas

Our aim in this book was to extend the justification for, and method of undertaking, comparative research in the interpretive tradition. Typically, when interpretivists compare they do so implicitly. They draw parallels or analogies between cases to help them understand their case. Nothing in this book contradicts attempts to undertake other types of comparison. But our primary rationale is that we compare because it is essential to providing 'decentred' explanations of the social world. The risk that more ideographic studies run is that context, however defined, becomes the de facto explanation for all social and political phenomena. If each case is the product of a particular history, and is locked in a particular language game, then this explains everything we need to know and considerably restricts any attempt to develop plausible conjectures that explain both similarities and differences.

We argue interpretive research using an abductive logic both starts with and refines plausible conjectures. We think an empirical focus on the dilemmas of human actors allows interpretivists to say when 'context matters' but also leaves open the possibility that some problems may well be universal, depending on how broadly we describe the dilemma. We say an empirical focus because we see this as the only possible way to answer the universal-particular question. But, we still wonder whether by using dilemmas to unlock the comparative potential of interpretive research, we require a level of abstraction that borders on banality and undermines the key strength of interpretive research: the ability to capture and communicate contextual subtleties and nuances. By seeking the universal in the particular, could we be interpreted as naturalising dilemmas even if this is not our aim?

Again, we hope not! We have repeatedly acknowledged the unavoidable and pragmatic trade-off between depth and breadth when undertaking and writing-up comparative interpretive research. In some instances, this trade-off may not be worth it, and we do not want to discourage researchers from undertaking single case studies. But, as outlined above, single case studies have limits, not just for naturalists but for humanists too. In response to persistent criticisms that their work is ideographic, the new area studies seeks to break out of the straightjacket of geography to study the intercon-nections between people and places (see Hodgett, in press). Even the 'lost' tribes of anthropology are increasingly seen less as atomised units located in a particular time and space that must be understood solely on their own terms, and more as parts of wider systems of exchange and knowledge production that share stronger and weaker affinities across societies and language groups (see Clifford and Marcus; 1986; Marcus 1995). Following these moves, if our aim as interpretivists is to provide decentred explan-ations that could plausibly speak to general themes, then we think the risk that comparing via dilemmas might flatten context is worth taking. Hope-fully our own work, and that of others who take a similar approach, will bear this hunch out.

The Dilemma of Selection

The final dilemma is an ethical one about how to present interpretive comparison. The idea of a novel approach to comparison, particularly one which allows us to make 'unlikely' comparisons like the village bus and island boat in Chapter 3, appeals to us because it allows us to speak to mainstream political science while pushing beyond informal taboos in the idiographic tradition. But, as we have stressed above, the taboos, and the traditional eschewal of the mainstream that come with them, are there for a reason. In area studies, the commitment to an idiographic approach is intimately entwined with a *political* struggle that rejects the rigid categorisa-tion of, and generalisation about, local contexts. Moreover, the methods of idiographic studies, which we also use as interpretivists, can reinforce these proclivities. By going into the field, we get to know participants, and we come to appreciate the subtleties and nuances of their particular circum-stances from their particular vantage point. Against this background, the practical work of drawing out interpretive comparison – the selection of quotes, the recalling of anecdotes, the juxtaposition of rich material from disparate contexts – can mean walking a fine line. The dilemma of selection entails balancing the professional (i.e. saying something interesting and consequential to colleagues), the political (i.e. the historical, social and political currents in the contexts where we research) and the personal (i.e. respect for the personal relationships built up in the field). We worry about being seen to flatten context, to belittle historical grievances, to find patterns that may not be meaningful to our participants. As with most ethical concerns in research, there is no right or wrong answer as to how to navigate these prerogatives; the rule of thumb is to practise professional reflexivity.

Our recounting of the village bus vignette in Chapter 3, for instance, throws this dilemma into relief. Boswell secured permission from the University of Southampton's ethics board before doing the research. As a result, some of the specific details have been altered or generalised to protect participant anonymity. But meeting the formal requirements – with which most academics will be familiar – is not where ethical consideration begins and ends. There are many additional things we could have said about the encounter with Edna that might have added layers of nuance, richness and intimacy. We could say more about her appearance, her accent and her fashion choices. We could say more about her flat, its surrounds and its decor. There were many more personal details we could have shared about her background, her upbringing, her marriage. These intimacies are at the heart of evocative writing. But Boswell did not think any of this would add to the story or its purpose in this book. He felt some of these details might distract from the central point about the village bus, setting off other associations for readers (for example, about the historical, social and political context of inequality and class in Britain). More important, he did not feel comfortable sharing everything, even suitably anonymised. He felt it risked betraying the warmth and trust of his interaction with Edna. Other researchers might have made other decisions, of course, but the point is that the dilemma of selection is integral to writing-up qualitative research, more obviously and acutely so in the comparative interpretive approach. So, while we forego one set of political commitments common to the more ideographic tradition, we acknowledge that our approach comes with its own ethical tensions too.

The Comparative Interpretive Toolkit

The final task then is to sum up our argument and contribution. Our argument, simply put, is that if interpretivists want to provide decentred explanations, they have to compare, and that the best way to do so is to start with the dilemmas that situated agents confront in their everyday lives. We defined dilemmas in Chapter 3 as: an idea that stands in contradiction to other beliefs, posing a problem. Dilemmas are resolved by accommodating the new belief in the present web of beliefs or replacing old beliefs with new beliefs. Having identified these dilemmas in particular contexts, we then see whether they share a family resemblance with other actors in different circumstances. In doing so, we can creatively explain similarities and differences between even the most unlikely of actors and situations, rendering the exotic familiar and the familiar exotic. This simple message is significant, because the tendency within existing research traditions is to either stifle or smother the comparative intuition that makes this type of analysis possible.

Naturalists, working from a logic of justification standpoint, compare by isolating and controlling for certain variables (e.g. economic, institutional, cultural, etc.). To do so they have to reify each in order to make their comparison feasible. They flatten context, run rough shod over nuance and contextual subtleties, but the payoff is theoretical parsimony. To be sure, this description is caricatured and represents the most extreme large-N quantitative analysis. But, by adopting the same logic of justification, even more qualitative orientated comparisons with a smaller N fit their studies into this language. Doing so stifles the comparative intuition, rendering it subservient to methodological rules that dictate what cases and procedures of data collection and analysis will allow them to test and falsify existing theories.

Humanists, by contrast, are more inclined to approach their work from a logic of discovery, entering the field with multiple theoretical puzzles and then following where they are led. Much of what we have written here is in sympathy with this approach. But, we also detect two common pitfalls with this type of research, both of which stem from a desire to capture as authentically as possible the nuance and subtleties of singular contexts. First, context becomes the de facto causal explanation for all socio-political phenomena because each instance is *sui generis*. Second, researchers struggle to see the wood through the trees, so their studies remain mired in detail. Both of these tendencies smother the comparative intuition. Again, this position is a caricature that represents the most extreme version of area studies. But we have also run afoul of this tendency ourselves, so know all too well how seductive a trap it can be.

Having set up these two orientations towards comparison, our vision for this book has been to chart a course unequivocally rooted in a humanist standpoint. To do so, we have started with interpretive theory as advanced by Bevir and Rhodes (summarised in Chapter 2). Specifically, we have utilised the concepts outlined in Table 8.1 as the philosophical foundation for our comparative approach.

But, Bevir and Rhodes do not specifically talk about comparison in their articulation of interpretive theory. What is more, they have tended to

Table 8.1 The interpretive approach: concepts

Concept	Definition
To decentre	To decentre is to unpack practices as the contingent beliefs and actions of individuals, challenging the idea that inexorable or impersonal forces drive politics.
Narratives	Narratives are a form of explanation that works by relating actions to individual beliefs and desires that produce them. This allows us to capture how events happened in the past or are happening today.
Situated agency	Individuals are situated in wider webs of beliefs (traditions), which largely shape their beliefs. Yet they keep a capacity for agency in that they respond to traditions, beliefs and dilemmas in novel ways.
Beliefs	Beliefs are the basic unit of analysis, in that they are the interpretations of individuals of their world and their surroundings.
Traditions	Traditions are 'webs of belief', and form the background of ideas in which agents find themselves. Agents will adopt beliefs from traditions as a starting point, but may amend them.
Dilemmas	A dilemma is an idea that stands in contradiction to other beliefs, posing a problem. Dilemmas are resolved by accommodating the new belief in the present web of beliefs or replacing old beliefs with new beliefs.
Practices	A set of actions that often exhibits a stable pattern across time. Practices are the ways in which beliefs and traditions manifest themselves in everyday life.

Source: Geddes and Rhodes (2018).

understate the importance of dilemmas in their empirical explanations relative to other concepts like tradition. This book provides an extension of their interpretive theory by explicitly outlining an approach to comparison for the first time. To do so we have placed the dilemmas of situated agents at the forefront of our approach. We have also created a distinct vocabulary for comparative interpretive research that we summarise in Table 8.2.

Comparative Intuition

Our starting point for this book, building on Anderson (2016), is the claim that comparison is intuitive. All of us, in our everyday lives, engage in 'constant comparison' in order to make sense of people, places and events as they unfold across time and space. The patterns we observe help us determine what is different or similar about a new experience. As scholars, we draw on implicit comparisons to help communicate ideas and make insights interesting for a broad audience. Therefore, because human beings are comparative animals, interpretivist scholars have much to gain by embracing this intuition. Indeed, we would argue that interpretive research is

Table 8.2 The comparative extension to the interpretive toolkit

Comparative extension	Description
Comparative intuition	We are comparative animals and so we all possess a comparative intuition. We also cannot decentre without comparing, even if it is only between rival accounts. There is thus considerable value in making that comparison explicit.
Big-C/Pro-C creativity	Comparing dilemmas is a creative act. It cannot be forced into the language of variables and controls common to research in the naturalist tradition – and even if it could we would not want to! Rather, we encourage researchers to seek out eclectic affinities between dilemmas.
Kaleidoscope	All agents are situated within multiple, intersecting social fields (age, gender, ethnicity, profession, etc.). The classic social science approach is to make each field the subject of empirical analysis. Starting with agents rather than fields allows us to see how dilemmas recur and intersect. The effect is akin to looking through a kaleidoscope, with the same practices and processes given new meaning depending on the agent narrating it.
Big-D/small-d dilemmas	The key to opening up the comparative potential of interpretive research is to focus on the dilemmas of situated agents. Dilemmas must be understood in context but they share a family resemblance that allows us to compare across contexts and tease out what is similar and different about each.
Puzzling	Puzzling describes the abductive logic that we employ when approaching our research topic. We puzzle about certain questions that lead us to the field. Once in the field we puzzle with our participants to make sense of the dilemmas they confront. As we write up we seek to make those puzzles intelligible to others.
Wood through the trees	The aim of our puzzling is to move through our data and in doing so render complex specificity in context intelligible to a wider audience. We say 'through the trees' because in our experience much in-depth interpretive research gets bogged down by the sheer volume of data entailed in this type of project.
Yo-yo fieldwork	Comparative interpretive research trades depth for breadth. We seek to reconcile this by moving in and out of the field, writing as we go, and sharing these drafts with research participants. It is not the same as conventional anthropological ethnography – nor is it meant to be!
Impressionistic analysis	When analysing, we explicitly acknowledge that our research also takes place in an academic field. Different aspects of our data will appeal to different audiences. Choices about which aspects of the empirics to emphasise and which to downplay for different outlets is an intensely creative task, akin to producing a work of impressionistic art.
Evocative writing	In addition to being factual and truthful, our writing seeks to evoke the everyday life and dilemmas of others by persuading readers they know these people and where they live.

uniquely placed to celebrate and cultivate the comparative intuition. Specifically, where naturalist approaches seek to discipline this intuition in the service of theoretical parsimony, and area studies scholars seek to deny it in favour of contextual subtlety, interpretive comparison is a vital means of both *understanding* and *conveying* context. It is only through comparison that new insights and experiences become meaningful, and can be communicated to relevant audiences.

Big-C/Pro-C Creativity

The comparative intuition is essential for undertaking creative, discovery-orientated research. We like Kaufman and Beghetto's (2009) distinction between Big-C creativity and Pro-C creativity. Our hope is that by releasing the methodological shackles and embracing our comparative intuition, daringly creative and discovery-orientated research will follow. The problem, as it currently stands, is that when such work does emerge – think of scholars like Scott or Anderson – the method by which it was developed is treated is a mysterious alchemy, unable to be replicated or repeated. This book aims to demystify that process. We have not provided an instruction manual. Rather, we have provided a guidebook based on lived experience – both ours and others – of doing this type of research. The centrepiece of this guidebook is the 'rules of thumb' that we have used to structure Chapters 3 to 7. We use the term 'rule of thumb' in its everyday meaning to describe a principle developed from practice.

Kaleidoscope

The main reason why we need to demystify the alchemy of creating comparative interpretive research is that comparison is central to the core interpretive aim of providing a decentred analysis of the social and political world. As we outlined in Chapter 2, to decentre is to unpack the contingent beliefs and actions of individuals, challenging the idea that inexorable or impersonal forces drive politics. Decentred explanations specify the beliefs and desires that cause actions. Because people act for reasons, we take their narration of their reasons seriously. When undertaking comparative research, the metaphor we adopt is that of a kaleidoscope. A kaleidoscope evokes different patterns depending on which web of beliefs and practices is the focus of attention. And yet, each distinct pattern is created from common or shared experiences. It is hewn from the same pieces. Viewing the political world through the eyes of situated agents allows us to see how social fields (age, gender, ethnicity, profession, etc.) intersect and produce dilemmas. By comparing the meanings, beliefs and practices of agents in different contexts, we can tease out what is similar and what is different. Context is thus always central to our explanation, but it is never our de facto explanation. Comparison and the interpretive project of decentring therefore go hand in hand.

Big-D/Small-d Dilemmas

Dilemmas are the intellectual skeleton key that unlocks the potential of comparative interpretive research. As we outlined in Chapter 3, we use the term dilemma in the particular analytical sense with which it is used in Bevir and Rhodes's (2003, 2006) account of interpretive theory (see Chapter 2). Their meaning is entirely consistent with the everyday sense of the term – that is, a dilemma entails making a choice between two or more alternative (and often undesirable) courses of action. With Big-D dilemmas, change occurs when new ideas alter established traditions. With small-d dilemmas, change occurs in everyday practices. In practice, this means that when we look through the kaleidoscope and ask why actors act, we create an opportunity for them to reflect on their choices. By reflecting *with* actors, we uncover the how they rationalise their actions. By understanding how they *see* these choices, as a reflection of the webs of belief in which they are embedded, we are able to explain why they do what they do. When we ask whether others experience the same dilemmas in a different context, we necessarily explore how their experience is either similar or different.

Puzzling

While dilemmas confront us in our empirical work, we do not enter the field without some pre-existing idea of what they might be. Rather, we start with a puzzle: something that confuses or excites us. As we outlined in Chapter 4, the puzzle informs where we start our project, but it does not dictate where we end up. Puzzling is a process with no clear destination; it is iterative and we change the puzzle as we seek to resolve our confusions, often multiple times over the course of a complex comparative project. Through deep, rigorous and continuous puzzling, interpretive scholars can feel emboldened to explore and tease out comparisons that surprise and intrigue, that uncover new insights or force readers to confront familiar insights in new ways. This emphasis on continual puzzling allows us to see old debates about research design and case selection in new ways. Specifically, we argue that case selection is not something that can be designed into a research project, but rather is something that emerges as we go, through an abductive conversation between theory and practice. We should therefore be open to changing, omitting or adding cases, either by ourselves or in collaboration with others.

Wood through the Trees

In Chapter 5, we employ two phrases to help researchers manage the depth–breadth trade-off inherent to undertaking comparative interpretive research. The first, seeing the 'wood through the trees', seeks to orientate us towards overcoming a common pitfall of interpretive research: that by focusing on rich idiographic detail, we lose sight of broader theoretical issues. We say wood *through* the trees rather than wood *for* the trees because the term *through* suggests that interpretivist researchers make knowledge claims only after passing *through* their fieldwork data. By approaching our data as something we puzzle *with* in order to pass *through* we can avoid this pitfall. The puzzle may never be fully 'resolved' in the naturalist sense of providing a definitive answer to a research question, but the aim is for its dimensions to become clearer and more intelligible to our chosen audiences. The mantra that we ultimately aim to see the wood through the trees captures a sense that we should keep our audience(s) in mind while we conduct fieldwork.

Yo-yo Fieldwork

The second phrase we invoke in Chapter 5 is 'yo-yo' fieldwork. Anthropological fieldwork is associated with the extended 'soak' or deep immersion. But, this is not practical for a single researcher undertaking a comparative project, and the pursuit of representativeness that this invokes is artificial anyway. To tease out similarities and differences between how actors experience dilemmas in different contexts, we argue that a more suitable approach is what Wulff (2002) calls 'yo-yo' fieldwork. So, we move in and out of the field, shifting between different sites, actors and data. By consciously and deliberately yo-yoing researchers can maximise the strengths of this approach because the experience of yo-yoing forces the researcher to make sense of what is recurring and what is context specific in the way actors experience and respond to dilemmas. It also enables them to reflect on when they have enough data from a field site or when they need to go back for more.

Impressionistic Analysis

To make sense of the mountain of data that comparative interpretive research inevitably produces we employ the term impressionistic analysis in Chapter 6. We do not use the term in the everyday sense of impressionistic – being vague, hastily reached or uninformed. Rather, we reclaim the meaning of impressionism as associated with the revolutionary art movement of the nineteenth century and its attempt to capture life in everyday settings *as they saw it*. Seen in this way, an impressionistic orientation is ideally suited to the particular challenges of conducting richly detailed comparative analysis. It is a stance that acknowledges that no analysis can do full justice to the complexities of social and political life. Rather it focuses our attention on the most striking features in the field – in comparative interpretive research, the dilemmas (and responses to dilemmas) we encounter are typically the vibrant dynamics that we seek to illuminate. As such, this orientation allows us to borrow across the established toolkits of qualitative analysis in ways that still entail and ensure richness, rigour and plausibility. But it also mitigates against the risks of analysis-by-paralysis that the humanist tradition of ill-defined 'indwelling' in particular can engender. Most importantly, in doing so, it provides appropriate licence to allow the analyst to embrace and enjoy the creative intuition at the core of comparative interpretive research.

Evocative Writing

Finally, in Chapter 7, we used the phrase evocative writing to describe how we bring the disparate parts of comparative interpretive research together. Rather than following a plan in which topic follows topic in an orderly sequence, we seek to evoke the everyday life and dilemmas of others by persuading readers they know these people and where they live. Such story-telling is akin to the art of the novel or the biography. Unlike fiction, however, our writing remains factual and 'truthful', even if the logic is not linear and at times resembles a continuous Penrose staircase forever looping back on itself.

In sum, our comparative extension to the interpretive toolkit has the advantages listed in Table 8.3.

Table 8.3 Advantages of a comparative interpretive approach

1. It embraces complex specificity in context (idiographic detail) yet seeks to make plausible conjectures (general statements), which open the possibility of theoretical innovation.
2. By making unlikely comparisons, it uncovers new research agendas and research questions.
3. It favours creativity over the protocols of naturalism, thereby admitting of surprises – of moments of epiphany, serendipity and happenstance – that can open new research agendas.
4. To understand dilemmas, it recovers the beliefs and practices of actors thus providing the texture, depth and nuance that gets behind the surface of official accounts.
5. By analysing the contradictions of everyday practices, it unearths the conflicting practices and contending narratives of actors in political and social life.
6. It allows us to frame (and reframe and reframe) questions in a way that recognises that our understandings about how things work around here evolves during the fieldwork.
7. Comparing dilemmas challenges existing concepts, generates novel understandings and redefines the political phenomena under study.
8. Comparative interpretive research encourages sharing research with academic colleagues and co-production with politicians, public servants and citizens.
9. Comparing beliefs, practices and dilemmas helps us to identify and analyse the symbolic, performative aspects of political action.
10. Comparative interpretive research encourages us to experiment in our writing to communicate with diverse audiences and to 'decrease our dullness'.

Source: Modified from Rhodes (2017b: 209); Simmons and Smith (2015)

We have presented a set of concepts and methods, backed up by practical rules of thumb, for undertaking comparative interpretive research. It may seem a tad eccentric to mainstream political scientists, but we insist it is a practical enterprise not another instance of epistemological debate. Not only is comparative interpretive research possible but fieldwork is also much more fun than sitting in the library.

Envoi

In the beginning, we quoted with approval Benedict Anderson's observation that comparison was revealing and produced surprises. We welcome also his observations on strangeness:

One has to be endlessly curious about everything, sharpen one's eyes and ears, and take notes about everything. The experience of strangeness makes all your senses more sensitive than normal, and your attachment to comparison grows deeper. This is why fieldwork is also so useful when you return home. You will have developed habits of observation and comparison that encourage or force you to start noticing that your own culture is just as strange. (Anderson 2016: 101–102)

Our book is an invitation to uncover strangeness at home and abroad and our rules of thumb are the map for the journey.

References

Abbott, A. (2004) *Methods of Discovery: Heuristics for the Social Sciences*. New York: WW Norton & Company.

Abu-Lughod, L. (2006) [1991] 'Writing against culture', in Moore, H. L. and Sanders, T. (eds.) *Anthropology in Theory: Issues in Epistemology*. Malden: Blackwell Publishing, pp. 466–479.

Adcock, R. (2006) 'Generalization in comparative and historical social science: the difference that interpretivism makes', in Yanow, D. and Schwartz-Shea, P. (eds.) *Interpretation and Method*. New York: Routledge, pp. 50–66.

Agar, M. (1996) [1980] *The Professional Stranger*, 2nd ed. San Diego: Academic Press.

Anderson, B. (1983) *Imagined Communities: Reflections on the Origin and Spread of Nationalism*, rev. ed. London: Verso.

(2016) *A Life beyond Boundaries*. London: Verso.

Bailey, F. G. (2001) [1969] *Stratagems and Spoils: A Social Anthropology of Politics*, new ed. Boulder, CO: Westview.

Barthes, R. (1970) 'The discourse of history', in Lane, M. (ed.) *Structuralism: A Reader*. London: Jonathan Cape, pp. 145–155.

Bates, R. H. (1997) 'Area studies and the discipline: a useful controversy?', *Political Science and Politics* 30 (2): 166–169.

Bayard de Volo, L. (2015) 'Comparative politics', in Bevir, M. and Rhodes, R. A. W. (eds.) *Routledge Handbook of Interpretive Political Science*. London/New York: Routledge, pp. 241–255.

Bennett, A. and Checkel, J. T. (eds.) (2015) *Process Tracing: From Metaphor to Analytic Tool*. Cambridge: Cambridge University Press.

Bevir, M. (1999) *The Logic of the History of Ideas*. Cambridge: Cambridge University Press.

Bevir, M. and Blakely, J. (2018) *Interpretive Social Science: An Anti-Naturalist Approach*. Oxford: Oxford University Press.

Bevir, M. and Kedar, A. (2008) 'Concept formation in political science: an anti-naturalist critique of qualitative methodology', *Perspectives on Politics* 6: 503–517.

Bevir, M. and Rhodes, R. A. W. (2003) *Interpreting British Governance*. London: Routledge.

(2006) *Governance Stories*. London: Routledge.

(2010) *The State as Cultural Practice*. Oxford: Oxford University Press.

(eds.) (2015) *The Routledge Handbook of Interpretive Political Science*. London: Routledge.

Blatter, J. and Haverland, M. (2012) *Designing Case Studies: Explanatory Approaches in Mall-N Research*. Houndmills, Basingstoke: Palgrave Macmillan.

Boin, A., 't Hart, P., Stern, E. and Sundelius, B. (2005) *The Politics of Crisis Management: Public Leadership under Pressure*. Cambridge: Cambridge University Press.

Booker, C. (2005) *The Seven Basic Plots: Why We Tell Stories*. London: Continuum.

Boswell, J. (2014) '"Hoisted with our own petard": evidence and democratic deliberation on obesity', *Policy Sciences* 47 (4): 345–365.

(2015) 'Toxic narratives in the deliberative system: how the ghost of Nanny stalks the obesity debate', *Policy Studies* 36 (3): 314–328.

(2016a) *The Real War on Obesity: Contesting Knowledge and Meaning in a Public Health Crisis*. Houndmills, Basingstoke: Palgrave Macmillan.

(2016b) 'Deliberating downstream: countering democratic distortions in the policy process', *Perspectives on Politics* 14 (3): 724–737.

(2018) 'What makes evidence-based policy making such a useful myth? The case of NICE guidance on bariatric surgery in the United Kingdom', *Governance* 31 (2): 199–214.

Boswell, J., Cairney, P. and St Denny, E. (2019) 'The politics of institutionalizing preventive health', *Social Science and Medicine* 228: 202–210.

Boswell, J. and Corbett, J. (2015a) 'Embracing impressionism: revealing the brush strokes of interpretive research', *Critical Policy Studies* 9: 216–225.

(2015b) 'Who are we trying to impress? Reflections on navigating political science, ethnography and interpretation', *Journal of Organizational Ethnography* 4 (2): 223–235.

(2015c) 'On making an impression: a response to our critics', *Critical Policy Studies* 9 (3): 375–379.

(2015d) 'Stoic Democrats? Anti-politics, elite cynicism and the policy process', *Journal of European Public Policy* 22 (10): 1388–1405.

(2017) 'Why and how to compare deliberative systems', *European Journal of Political Research* 56 (4): 801–819.

Boswell, J., Hendriks, C. M. and Ercan, S. A. (2016) Message received? Examining transmission in deliberative systems. *Critical Policy Studies* 10 (3): 263–283.

Boswell, J., Ryan, M., Killick, A., et al. (2018) *Making Ends Meet: Experiencing Deprivation on the South Coast of England*. York: Joseph Rowntree Foundation.

Boudon, R. (1993) 'Towards a synthetic theory of rationality', *International Studies in the Philosophy of Science* 7: 5–19.

Braa, J., Monteiro, E. and Sahay, S. (2004) 'Networks of action: sustainable health information systems across developing countries', *MIS Quarterly* 28 (3): 337–362.

Brady, H. E. and Collier, D. (eds.) (2010) *Rethinking Social Inquiry: Diverse Tools, Shared Standards*. 2nd rev. ed. New York: Rowman & Littlefield Publishers.

Braun, V. and Clarke, V. (2006) 'Using thematic analysis in psychology', *Qualitative Research in Psychology*, 3: 77–101.

Bryman, A. (ed.) (2001) *Ethnography*. Volume 1: *The Nature of Ethnography*; Volume 2: *Ethnographic Fieldwork Practice*; Volume 3: *Issues in Ethnography*; Volume 4: *Analysis and Writing in Ethnography*. London: Sage Benchmarks in Social Research Methods.

Burawoy, A. (1998) 'The extended case method', *Sociological Theory* 16: 4–33.

Burns, T. (1977) *The BBC: Public Institution and Private World*. London: Macmillan.

Carnap, R. (1937) *The Logical Syntax of Language*. London: Routledge & Kegan Paul.

Charmaz, K. (2006) *Constructing Grounded Theory: A Practical Guide through Qualitative Analysis.* London: Sage.

Clancy, J. I. (ed.) (2003) *Impressionism: Historical Overview and Bibliography.* New York: Nova Science.

Clifford, J. (1986) 'Introduction: partial truths', in Clifford, J. and Marcus G. E. (eds.) *Writing Culture: The Poetics and Politics of Ethnography.* Berkeley: University of California Press, pp. 1–26.

   (1988) 'On ethnographic authority', in *The Predicament of Culture. Twentieth Century Ethnography, Literature, and Art.* Cambridge, MA: Harvard University Press, pp. 21–54.

Clifford, J. and Marcus, G. E. (eds.) (1986) *Writing Culture. The Poetics and Politics of Ethnography.* Berkeley: University of California Press.

Collier, D., Brady, H. E. and Seawright, J. (2010) 'Critiques, responses and trade offs: drawing together the debate', in Brady, H. E. and Collier, D. (eds.) *Rethinking Social Inquiry: Diverse Tools, Shared Standards,* 2nd rev. ed. New York: Rowman & Littlefield Publishers, pp. 195–227.

Collini, S. (2012) *What Are Universities For?* London: Penguin Books.

Coppedge, M. (2012) *Democratization and Research Methods.* Cambridge: Cambridge University Press.

Corbett, J. (2012) '"Two worlds"? Interpreting political leadership narratives in the 20th-century Pacific', *The Journal of Pacific History* 47: 69–91.

   (2013a) 'Politicians and professionalization in the Pacific Islands: revisiting self-regulation?', *Politics & Policy* 41 (6): 852–876.

   (2013b) '"A calling from God": politicians and religiosity in the Pacific Islands', *Global Change, Peace & Security* 25 (3): 283–297.

   (2014) 'Practising reflection: empathy, emotion and intuition in political life writing', *Life Writing* 11: 349–365.

   (2015a) *Being Political: Leadership and Democracy in the Pacific Islands.* Honolulu: University of Hawai'i Press.

   (2015b) '"Everybody knows everybody": practising politics in the Pacific Islands', *Democratization* 22 (1): 51–72.

   (2015c) 'Small fish swimming in the shape of a shark: why politicians join political parties in the Pacific Islands', *Commonwealth & Comparative Politics* 53 (2): 130–152.

   (2017) *Australia's Foreign Aid Dilemma: Humanitarian Aspirations Confront Democratic Legitimacy.* London: Routledge.

Corbett, J. and Liki, A. (2015) 'Intersecting identities, divergent views: interpreting the experiences of women politicians in the Pacific Islands', *Politics & Gender* 11: 320–344.

Corbett, J. and Shiu, R. N. (2014) 'Leadership succession and the high drama of political conduct: corruption stories from Samoa', *Pacific Affairs* 87 (4): 743–763.

Corbett, J. and Veenendaal, W. (2016) 'Westminster in small states: comparing the Caribbean and Pacific experience', *Contemporary Politics* 22 (4): 432–449.

   (2018) *Democracy in Small States: Why It Can Persist Against All Odds.* Oxford: Oxford University Press.

Corbett, J., Veenendaal, W. and Ugyel, L. (2017) 'Why monarchy persists in small states: the cases of Tonga, Bhutan and Liechtenstein', *Democratization* 24 (4): 689–706.

Corbett, J. and Wood, T. (2013) 'Profiling politicians in Solomon Islands: professionalisation of a political elite?' *Australian Journal of Political Science* 48 (3): 320–334.

Coser, L. A. (1974) *Greedy Institutions: Patterns of Undivided Commitment*. New York: The Free Press.

Cramer, K. J. (2012) 'Putting inequality in its place: rural consciousness and the power of perspective', *American Political Science Review* 106 (3): 517–532.

(2016) *The Politics of Resentment: Rural Consciousness in Wisconsin and the Rise of Scott Walker*. Chicago: University of Chicago Press.

Crewe, E. (2005) *Lords of Parliament: Manners, Rituals and Politics*. Manchester: Manchester University Press.

Czarniawska, B. (2004) *Narratives in Social Science Research*. London: Sage.

Dasandi, N. and Erez, L. (2017) 'The donor's dilemma: international aid and human rights violations', *British Journal of Political Science* 1–22.

Delamont, S. (2007) 'Ethnography and participant observation', in Seale, C., Giampietri, G., Gubrium, J. F. and Silverman D. S. (eds.) *Qualitative Research Practice*. Thousand Oaks, CA: Sage, pp. 205–227.

Dexter, L. (2006) [1970] *Elite and Specialized Interviewing*. Colchester, Essex: European Consortium for Political Research.

Dowding, K. (2016) *The Philosophy and Methods of Political Science*. London: Palgrave.

Eckstein, H. (1975) 'Case studies and theory in political science', in Greenstein, F. and Polsby, N. (eds.) *Handbook of Political Science*, Vol. 7. Reading, MA: Addison-Wesley, pp. 94–137.

Ellis, C. (2004) *The Ethnographic I: A Methodological Novel about Autoethnography*. Walnut Creek, CA: AltaMira Press.

Ellis, C. and Bochner, A. P. (2000) 'Autoethnography, personal narratives and reflexivity: researcher as subject', in Denzin, N. K. and Lincoln, Y. S. (eds.) *Handbook of Qualitative Research*, 2nd ed. London: Sage, pp. 733–768.

(2006) 'Analyzing analytic autoethnography', *Journal of Contemporary Ethnography* 35: 429–449.

Elman, C. and Kapiszewski, D. (2014) 'Data access and research transparency in the qualitative tradition', *PS: Political Science & Politics* 47 (1): 43–47.

Elman, C., Kapiszewski, D. and Lupia, A. (2018) 'Transparent social inquiry: implications for political science', *Annual Review of Political Science* 21 (1): 29–47.

Emerson, R. M., Fretz, R. I. and Shaw, L. L. (2011) [1995] *Writing Ethnographic Field Notes*, 2nd ed. Chicago: University of Chicago Press.

Ercan, S. A. (2015) 'Creating and sustaining evidence for "failed multiculturalism": the case of "honor killing" in Germany', *American Behavioral Scientist* 59 (6): 658–678.

Ercan, S. A., Hendriks, C. M. and Boswell, J. (2017) 'Studying public deliberation after the systemic turn: the crucial role for interpretive research', *Policy and Politics* 45 (2): 195–212.

Fenno, R. F. (1978) *Home Style: House Members in their Districts*. Boston, MA: Little, Brown.

(1990) *Watching Politicians: Essays on Participant Observation*. Berkeley, CA: Institute of Governmental Studies, University of California.

Feyerabend, P. (1988) *Against Method*. Rev. ed. London: Verso.

Flinders, M. (2013) 'The tyranny of relevance and the art of translation', *Political Studies Review* 11: 149–167.

Flyvbjerg, B. (1998) *Rationality and Power: Democracy in Practice*. Chicago: University of Chicago Press.

(2006) 'Five misunderstandings about case studies', *Qualitative Inquiry* 12: 219–245.

Fujii, L. A. (2013) 'The puzzle of extra-lethal violence', *Perspectives on Politics* 11: 410–426.

(2017) *Interviewing in Social Science Research: A Relational Approach*. Abingdon, Oxon and New York: Routledge.

Fox, K. (2004) *Watching the English. The Hidden Rules of English Behaviour*. London: Hodder & Stoughton.

Furlong, P. and Marsh, D. (2002) 'Skin not a sweater: ontology and epistemology in political science', in Marsh, D. and Stoker, G.(eds.) *Theory and Methods in Political Science*. Houndmills, Basingstoke: Palgrave Macmillan, pp. 17–41.

Gadamer, H. (1960) *Truth and Method*. Translated by Weinscheimer, J. and Marshall, D. G. Reprinted 2004. New York: Continuum.

Geddes, M. (2018) 'The explanatory potential of "dilemmas": bridging practices and power to understand political change in interpretive political science', *Political Studies Review* https://doi.org/10.1177/1478929918795342.

Geddes, M. and Rhodes, R. A. W. (2018) 'Towards an interpretive parliamentary studies', in Brichzin, J., Krichewsky, D., Ringel, L. and Schank, J. (eds.) *The Sociology of Parliaments*. Wiesbaden: Springer VS, pp. 87–107.

Gee, J.P. (2004) *An Introduction to Discourse Analysis: Theory and Method*. London: Routledge.

Geertz, C. (1973) 'Thick description: toward an interpretive theory of culture', In his *The Interpretation of Cultures*. New York: Basic Books, pp. 3–30.

(1980) *Negara: The Theatre State in Nineteenth Century Bali*. Princeton, NJ: Princeton University Press.

(1983) 'Blurred genres: the refiguration of social thought', In his *Local Knowledge: Further Essays in Interpretive Anthropology*. New York: Basic Books, pp. 19–35.

(1988) *Works and Lives: The Anthropologist as Author*. Stanford: Stanford University Press.

(2001) 'The state of the art', in his *Available Light. Anthropological Reflections on Philosophical Topics*, 3rd paperback ed. Princeton, NJ: Princeton University Press, pp. 89–142.

George, A. L. and Bennett, A. (2005) *Case Studies and Theory Development in the Social Sciences*. Cambridge, MA: MIT Press.

Gerring, J. (2004) 'What is a case study and what is it good for?', *American Political Science Review* 98: 341–354.

(2006) *Case Study Research: Principles and Practices*. Cambridge: Cambridge University Press.

(2007) 'Is there a (viable) crucial-case method?', *Comparative Political Studies* 40: 231–253.

(2012a) *Social Science Methodology: A Unified Framework*, 2nd ed. Cambridge: Cambridge University Press.

(2012b) 'Mere description', *British Journal of Political Science* 42(4): 721–746.

(2017) 'Qualitative methods', *Annual Review of Political Science* 20: 15–36.

Geuijen, K., 't Hart, P. and Yesilkagit, K. (2007) 'Dutch eurocrats at work: getting things done in Europe', in Rhodes, R. A. W., 't Hart, P. and Noordegraaf, M. (eds.) *Observing Government Elites: Up Close and Personal*. Houndmills, Basingstoke: Palgrave-Macmillan, pp. 131–159.

Gibson-Graham, J.-K. (2004) 'Area studies after Poststructuralism', *Environment and Planning* A36 (3): 405–419.

Giddens, A. (1993) *New Rules of Sociological Method: A Positive Critique of Interpretive Sociologies*, 2nd ed. with a new Introduction. Cambridge: Polity Press.

Glaser, B. G. and Strauss, A. L. (2017) [1967] *The Discovery of Grounded Theory: Strategies for Qualitative Research*. Abingdon, Oxon: Routledge.

Goertz, G. (2006) *Social Science Concepts: A User's Guide*. Princeton, NJ:Princeton University Press.

Goertz, Gary, and James Mahoney. (2012) *A Tale of Two Cultures: Qualitative and Quantitative Research in the Social Sciences*. Princeton, NJ: Princeton University Press.

Goodsell, C. T. (1988) *The Social Meaning of Civic Space: Studying Political Authority through Architecture*. Lawrence: University Press of Kansas.

  (2001) *The American Statehouse: Interpreting Democracy's Temples* . Lawrence: University Press of Kansas.

Greaves, J. and Grant, W. (2010) 'Crossing the interdisciplinary divide: political science and biological science', *Political Studies* 58 (2): 320–339.

Greenhalgh, T., Russel, J., Ashcroft, R. and Parsons, W. (2011) 'Why national health programs need dead philosophers: wittgensteinian reflections on policymakers' reluctance to learn from history', *Milbank Quarterly* 89: 533–563.

Habermas, J. (1989) *The Structural Transformation of the Public Sphere: An Inquiry into a Category of Bourgeois Society*. Cambridge, MA: MIT Press.

Haggard, S. and Kaufman, R. R. (2016), 'Democratization during the third wave', *Annual Review of Political Science* 19: 125–144.

Hajer, M. A. (1996) *The Politics of Environmental Discourse: Ecological Modernization and the Policy Process*. New ed. Oxford: Oxford University Press.

  (2009) *Authoritative Governance: Policy Making in the Age of Mediatization*. Oxford: Oxford University Press.

Hammersley, M. (1990) *Reading Ethnographic Research: A Critical Guide*. Harlow, Essex: Longman.

Hammersley, M. and Atkinson, P. (2007) [1983] *Ethnography: Principles in Practice*, 3rd ed. London: Routledge.

Hay, C. (2011) 'Interpreting interpretivism interpreting interpretations: the new hermeneutics of public administration', *Public Administration* 89: 167–182.

  (2017) 'Explanation, prediction, causation – an unholy trinity? Appreciative comments on the philosophy and methods of political science', *Political Studies Review* 15: 180–186.

Heclo, H. (2010) [1974] *Modern Social Politics in Britain and Sweden*. Washington DC: Rowman & Littlefield International for the ECPR Press.

Hendriks, C. M. (2007) 'Praxis stories: experiencing interpretive policy research', *Critical Policy Analysis* 1: 278–300.

  (2016) 'Coupling citizens and elites in deliberative systems: the role of institutional design', *European Journal of Political Research* 55 (1): 43–60.

  (2017) 'Citizen-led democratic reform: innovations in Indi', *Australian Journal of Political Science* 52 (4): 481–499.

Herbert, R. E. (1988) *Impressionism: Art, Leisure and Parisian Society*. New Haven: Yale University Press.

Hodgett, S. (in press) '21st Century area studies: blurring genres, evolutionary thought and the production of theory', in Milutinovic, Z. (ed.) *The Rebirth of Area Studies: Challenges for History, Politics and International Relations in the 21st Century*. London: I.B. Tauris.

Hodgett, S. and Rhodes, R. A. W. (eds.) (in press) *What Political Science Can Learn from the Humanities: Blurring Genres*. Houndmills, Basingstoke: Palgrave Macmillan.

Isaac, J. C. (2015) 'For a more public political science', *Perspectives on Politics* 13 (2): 269–283.

Iusmen, I. and Boswell, J. (2017) 'The dilemmas of pursuing "throughput legitimacy" through participatory mechanisms', *West European Politics* 40 (2): 459–478.

Kapiszewski, D., Maclean, L. M. and Read, B. L. (2015) *Field Research in Political Science*. Cambridge: Cambridge University Press.

Kaufman, J. C. and Beghetto, R. A. (2009) 'Beyond big and little: the four C model of creativity', *Review of General Psychology* 13 (1): 1–12.

King, G., Keohane, R. O and Verba, S. (1994) *Designing Social Inquiry: Scientific Inference in Qualitative Research*. Princeton, NJ: Princeton University Press.

Klüver, H. (2009) 'Measuring interest group influence using quantitative text analysis', *European Union Politics* 10 (4): 535–549.

Kozbelt, A., Beghetto, R. A. and Runco, M. A. (2010) 'Theories of creativity', in Kaufman J. C. and Sternberg R. J. (eds.) *The Cambridge Handbook of Creativity*. Cambridge: Cambridge University Press, pp. 20–47.

Kvale, S. and Brinkmann, S. (2009) *Interviews: Learning the Craft of Qualitative Research*. California: Sage.

Law, J. (1994) 'Organization, narrative and strategy', in Hassard, J. and Parker, M. (eds.) *Towards a New Theory of Organizations*. London: Routledge, pp. 248–268.

(2004) *After Method: Mess in Social Science Research*. Abingdon, Oxon: Routledge.

Levi-Strauss, C. (1966) *The Savage Mind*. London: Weidenfeld and Nicolson.

Lijphart, A. (1971) 'Comparative politics and the comparative method', *American Political Science Review* 65 (3): 682–693.

(1985)*Power-Sharing in South Africa* (Berkeley: Institute of International Studies, University of California).

Lincoln, Y. S. and Guba, E. G. (1985) *Naturalistic Inquiry*. Newbury Park, CA: Sage.

Lubet, S. (2018) *Interrogating Ethnography: Why Evidence Matters*. Oxford: Oxford University Press.

Lupia, A. and Elman, C. (2014) 'Openness in political science: data access and research transparency: Introduction', *PS: Political Science & Politics* 47 (1): 19–42.

MacIntyre, A. (1972) 'Is a science of comparative politics possible?', in Laslett, P., Runciman, W. G. and Skinner, Q. (eds.) *Philosophy, Politics and Society*, 4th series. Oxford: Blackwell, pp. 8–26.

(2007) *After Virtue: A Study in Moral Theory*, 3rd rev. ed. Notre Dame, IN: University of Notre Dame Press.

Mackay, F. and Rhodes, R. A. W. (2013) 'Gender, greedy institutions and the departmental court', *Public Administration* 91: 582–598.

Malpass, J. (2013) 'Hans-George Gadamer', In *The Stanford Encyclopaedia of Philosophy*. https://plato.stanford.edu/entries/gadamer/ (accessed 5 March 2018).

Marcus, G. E. (1995) 'Ethnography in/of the world system: the emergence of multi-sited ethnography', *Annual Review in Anthropology* 24: 95–117.

Maynard-Moody, S. and Musheno, M. (2000) 'State agent or citizen agent: two narratives of discretion', *Journal of Public Administration Research and Theory* 10 (2): 329–358.

   (2003) *Cops, Teachers, Counselors: Stories from the Front Lines of Public Service*. Ann Arbor, Michigan: The University of Michigan Press.

McFarlane, C. and Robinson, J. (2012) 'Introduction: experiments in comparative urbanism', *Urban Geography* 33: 765–773.

Newman, J. and Clarke, J. (2009) *Publics, Politics and Power: Remaking the Public in Public Services*. London: Sage.

Oakeshott, M. (1996) *The Politics of Faith and the Politics of Scepticism*. Edited by T. Fuller. New Haven: Yale University Press.

O'Malley, E. (2011) 'Review of Comparing Westminster by R. A. W. Rhodes, John Wanna and Patrick Weller', *Political Studies Review* 9: 67–141.

Orr, K. and Bennett, M. (2009) 'Reflexivity in the co-production of academic-practitioner research', *Qualitative Research in Organizations and Management: An International Journal* 4(1): 85–102.

Ospina, S. and Dodge, J. (2005) 'Narrative inquiry and the search for connectedness: practitioners and academics developing public administration scholarship', *Public Administration Review* 65 (4): 409–423.

Pachirat, T. (2011) *Every Twelve Seconds: Industrialized Slaughter and the Politics of Sight*. New Haven: Yale University Press.

Perry, S. K. (1999) *Writing in Flow: Keys to Enhanced Creativity*. Writer's Digest Books. www.writersdigest.com/.

Polanyi, M. (1958) *Personal Knowledge: Towards a Post-Critical Philosophy*. London: Routledge.

Popper, K. (1959) *The Logic of Scientific Discovery*. New York: Basic Books.

Pouliot, V. (2014) 'Practice tracing', in his *Process Tracing: From Metaphor to Analytic Tool*. Cambridge: Cambridge University Press, pp. 237–259.

   (2016) *International Pecking Orders: The Politics and Practice of Multilateral Diplomacy*. Cambridge: Cambridge University Press.

Punch, M. (1986) *The Politics and Ethics of Fieldwork*. Newbury Park, CA: Sage.

Rabinowitz, D. (2014) 'Resistance and the city', *History and Anthropology* 25 (4): 472–487.

Ragin, C. C. (2009) *Redesigning Social Inquiry: Fuzzy Sets and Beyond*. Chicago: University of Chicago Press.

Rawnsley, A. (2001) *Servants of the People: The Inside Story of New Labour*, rev. ed. London: Penguin Books.

Reeher, G. (2006) *First Person Political: Legislative Life and the Meaning of Public Service*. New York: NYU Press.

Rhodes, R. A. W. (1975) The Councillor, Information and Urban Deprivation. Report to the Home Office, July 1975.

   (2011) *Everyday Life in British Government*. Oxford: Oxford University Press.

   (2016) 'Recovering the craft of public administration', *Public Administration Review* 76 (4): 638–647.

   (2017) *Interpretive Political Science*. Oxford: Oxford University Press.

Rhodes, R. A. W. and Tiernan, A. (2014) *The Gatekeepers*. Melbourne: Melbourne University Press.

Rhodes, R. A. W., Wanna, J. and Weller, P. (2009) *Comparing Westminster*. Oxford: Oxford University Press.

Ricci, D. (1984) *The Tragedy of Political Science: Politics, Scholarship, and Democracy*. New Haven: Yale University Press.

Richardson, L. (2000) 'Evaluating Ethnography', *Qualitative Inquiry* 6: 253–255.

Roberts, B. (2002) *Biographical Research*. Buckingham: Open University Press.

Robinson, J. (2011) 'Cities in a world of cities: the comparative gesture', *International Journal of Urban and Regional Research* 5 (1):1–23.

Rorty, R. (1980) *Philosophy and the Mirror of Nature*. Oxford: Blackwell.

Sanjek, R. (1990) *Fieldnotes: The Making of Anthropology*. Ithaca: Cornell University Press.

Savoie, D. (1999) *Governing from the Centre*. Toronto: Toronto University Press.

  (2008) *Court Government and the Collapse of Accountability in Canada and the United Kingdom*. Toronto: University of Toronto Press.

Schaffer, F. C. (2008) *The Hidden Costs of Clean Election Reform*. Ithaca: Cornell University Press.

  (2015) *Elucidating Social Science Concepts: An Interpretivist Guide*. London: Routledge.

Schmitter, P. C. (2009) 'The nature and future of comparative politics', *European Political Science Review* 1: 33–61.

Schwartz-Shea, P. and Yanow, D. (2012) *Interpretive Research Design: Concepts and Processes*. London: Routledge.

  (2016) 'Legitimizing political science or splitting the discipline? Reflections on DA-RT and the policy-making role of a professional association', *Politics & Gender* 12 (3): E11. DOI:10.1017/S1743923X16000428

Scott, J. C. (1979) *The Moral Economy of the Peasant: Rebellion and Subsistence in Southeast Asia*. New Haven: Yale University Press.

  (1985) *Weapons of the Weak: Everyday Forms of Peasant Resistance*. New Haven: Yale University Press.

  (1990) *Domination and the Arts of Resistance: Hidden Transcripts*. New Haven: Yale University Press.

  (2013) 'Crops, Towns, Governments', *London Review of Books* 35 (22): 13–15.

Seawright, J. and Gerring, J.(2008) 'Case selection techniques in case study research: a menu of qualitative and quantitative options', *Political Research Quarterly* 61: 294–308.

Simmons, E. S. and Smith, N. R. (2015) 'The case for comparative ethnography', *Qualitative and Multi-Method Research* 13 (2): 13–18. (We consulted the manuscript version accepted for *Comparative Politics* to be published in 2019.)

  (2017) 'Comparison with an ethnographic sensibility', *PS: Political Science & Politics* 50: 126–130.

Soss, J. (2002) *Unwanted Claims: The Politics of Participation in the US Welfare System*. Ann Arbor, Michigan: University of Michigan Press.

  (2018) 'On the varied uses of concepts in interpretive research', in Schaffer, F. C. (ed.) Symposium on Elucidating Social Science Concepts, *European Political Science* 17 (2): 319–324.

Soss, J., and Schram, S. F. (2007) 'A public transformed? Welfare reform as policy feedback', *American Political Science Review*, 101(1), 111–127.

Stone, D. (2016) 'Quantitative analysis as narrative', in Bevir, M. and Rhodes, R. A. W. (eds.) *Routledge Handbook of Interpretive Political Science*. New York: Routledge, pp. 157–170.

Sullivan, H. (2016) 'Interpretivism and public policy research', in Turnbull, N. (ed.) *Interpreting Governance, High Politics, and Public Policy*. London: Routledge, pp. 184–204.

Swales, J. M. and Feak, C. B. (2004) *Academic Writing for Graduate Students: Essential Tasks and Skills*, Vol. 1. Ann Arbor, MI: University of Michigan Press.

Taylor, C. (2010) [1985] *Philosophical Papers. Volume 1. Human Agency and Language*. Cambridge: Cambridge University Press.

t' Hart, P. (2007) 'Spies at the crossroads: observing change in the Dutch intelligence service', in Rhodes, R. A. W., 't Hart P. and Noordegraaf, M. (eds.) *Observing Government Elites: Up Close and Personal*. Houndmills, Basingstoke: Palgrave-Macmillan, pp. 51–77.

Turnbull, N. (2016b) 'Narrative and interpretive theory', in Ansell, C. and Torfing, J. (eds.) *Handbook on Governance*. Cheltenham: Edward Elgar, pp. 380–391.

van Maanen, J. (1988) *Tales of the Field: On Writing Ethnography*. Chicago: University of Chicago Press.

   (2010) 'A song for my supper: more tales of the field', *Organizational Research Methods* 13: 240–255.

Veenendaal, W. P. and Corbett, J. (2015) 'Why small states offer important answers to large questions', *Comparative Political Studies* 48: 527–549.

Vrasti, W. (2008) 'The strange case of ethnography and international relations', *Millennium: Journal of International Studies* 37: 279–301.

Wagenaar, H. (2011) *Meaning in Action: Interpretation and Dialogue in Policy Analysis*. New York: M. E. Sharpe.

   (2012) 'Dwellers on the threshold of practice: the interpretivism of Bevir and Rhodes', *Critical Policy Studies* 6: 85–99.

   (2016) 'Extending interpretivism: articulating the practice dimension in Bevir and Rhodes's differentiated polity model', in N. Turnbull (ed.) *Interpreting Governance, High Politics, and Public Policy*. New York: Routledge, pp. 133–150.

Wedeen, L. (2007) 'The Politics of deliberation: Qāt chews as public spheres in Yemen.' *Public Culture* 19 (1): 59–84.

   (2010) 'Reflections on ethnographic work in political science', *Annual Review of Political Science* 13: 255–272.

Weiss, R. S. (1995) *Learning from Strangers: The Art and Method of Qualitative Interview Studies*. New York: Simon and Schuster.

Wesley-Smith, T and Goss, J. (2010) *Remaking Area Studies: Teaching and Learning across Asia and the Pacific*. Honolulu: University of Hawaii Press.

White, H. (1973) *Metahistory*. Baltimore: Johns Hopkins University Press.

   (1987) *The Content of the Form*. Baltimore: Johns Hopkins University Press.

Wildavsky, A. (2010) [1993] *Craftways: On the Organization of Scholarly Work*. New Brunswick, NJ: Transaction Publishers.

Winch, P. (2002) *The Idea of a Social Science: And Its Relation to Philosophy*, 2nd ed. London: Routledge.

Wittgenstein, L. (2009) [1953] *Philosophical Investigations*, 4th ed. Edited by P. M. S. Hacker and J. Schulte. Oxford: Wiley-Blackwell.

Wolcott, H. F. (1995) *The Art of Fieldwork*. Walnut Creek, CA: Altamira Press.

Wolgast, E. (1992) *Ethics of an Artificial Person: Lost Responsibility in Professions and Organisations*. Stanford, CA: Standford University Press.

Wood, E. J. (2007) 'Field research', in Boix, C. and Stokes, S. C. (eds.) *The Oxford Handbook of Comparative Politics*. Oxford: Oxford University Press, pp. 123–146.

Worley, R. M., Worley, V. B. and Wood, B. A. (2016) 'There were ethical dilemmas all day long!': harrowing tales of ethnographic researchers in criminology and criminal justice', *Criminal Justice Studies* 29 (4): 289–308.

Wulff, H. (2002) 'Yo-Yo fieldwork: mobility and time in multi-local study of dance in Ireland', *Anthropological Journal of European Cultures* 11: 117–136.

Yanow, D. (2006) 'Neither rigorous nor objective? Interrogating criteria for knowledge claims in interpretive science', in Yanow, D. and Schwartz-Shea, P. (eds.) *Interpretation and Method: Empirical Research Methods and the Interpretive Turn*. ME Sharpe: New York, pp. 129–151.

(2009) 'Dear author, dear reader: the third hermeneutic in writing and reviewing ethnography', in Schatz, E. (ed.) *Political Ethnography*. Chicago, University of Chicago Press, pp. 275–302.

(2013) 'How built spaces mean', in Yanow, D. and Schwartz-Shea, P. (eds.) *Interpretation and Method: Empirical Research Methods and the Interpretive Turn*, 2nd ed. Armonk, NY: M. E. Sharpe, pp. 368–386.

Yanow D. (2014) 'Interpretive analysis and comparative research', in Engeli, I. and Allison, C.R. (eds.) *Comparative Policy Studies*. London: Palgrave Macmillan, pp. 131–159.

Yanow, D. and Schwartz-Shea, P. (2006) (eds.) *Interpretation and Method: Empirical Research Methods and the Interpretive Turn*. Armonk, NY: M. E. Sharpe.

Yin, R. K. (2014) *Case Study Research*, 5th ed. Thousand Oaks, CA: Sage.

Zacka, B. (2017) *When the State Meets the Street: Public Service and Moral Agency*. Cambridge, MA: The Belknap Press of Harvard University Press.

Index